# LESSONS FROM THE
# *FIGHTING COMMANDOS*

## Fred Neff
### Photographs by James Reid
### and Patrick O'Leary

**WITHDRAWN**

⌐ **Lerner Publications Company • Minneapolis**

To Major Barney Neff, fighter pilot, master of self-defense, and humanitarian, whose unselfish kindness and devotion to helping other people made the world a little bit better place

The models photographed in this book are Christa Neff, Richard DeValerio, Jim Reid, William McLeod, Elias Murdock, Helena Koudelka, and Peter Koudelka.

Japanese calligraphy on back cover by Kenichi Tazawa.

Copyright © 1995 by Lerner Publications Company

Library of Congress Cataloging-in-Publication Data
Neff, Fred.
    Lessons from the fighting commandos / by Fred Neff ; photographs
by James Reid and Patrick O'Leary.
        p.  cm.
    Includes index.
    ISBN 0-8225-1165-7 : $14.95
    1. Self-defense—Juvenile literature. 2. Martial arts—Juvenile
literature. I. Title.
GV1111.N4S25  1995
613.6'6—dc20                                              93-25391
                                                              CIP
                                                              AC

Manufactured in the United States of America
1  2  3  4  5  6  - I/SF -  00  99  98  97  96  95

# CONTENTS

# PREFACE

When I was a small boy, my uncle, Major Barney Neff, introduced me to the wonders of the fighting arts. He took me regularly to the gym, and I watched as he taught the intricacies of self-defense. The most mundane fighting techniques were graceful and effective as he taught them. All who learned from him were extremely fortunate. Equally important, he set an example of quiet confidence, not bragging or showing off his skill in his private life. He demonstrated the knowledge, strength, skill, and concern for others of a true master of self-defense.

A full history of Major Barney Neff could itself easily fill the pages of a very large book and is beyond the scope of this work. A very abbreviated outline of his background is, however, appropriate at the beginning of this book, *Lessons from the Fighting Commandos,* since he acted as the inspiration for the book.

Major Barney Neff was born in 1918 in St. Paul, Minnesota. As a young person, he was an outstanding all-around athlete. He enlisted in the U.S. Navy at the beginning of World War II. As an enlisted person, he boxed first as a light heavyweight and then as a heavyweight. Barney Neff won championships in both weight classes. Later, he served as a drill and boxing instructor. In December of 1942,

*Major Barney Neff*              Courtesy of the author

he became a naval officer cadet. He subsequently served as a Marine Corps test pilot for dive bombers and fighter planes. Later, he was transferred to the Pacific theater as a fighter pilot. After the war ended in 1945, he served as a pilot stationed in Hawaii. During this period he was active in the Marine Corps boxing program. Barney Neff also continued to study and practice commando fighting methods drawn from both Eastern and Western sources.

He supervised a training program for flight officers in boxing, self-defense, and survival training while serving in Hawaii. In 1946 he was honorably discharged from active service. He then served in the Marine Corps Reserve as a fighter pilot with the rank of major. In civilian life he participated in boxing as a trainer, referee, cutman, and administrator. Major Neff trained many successful professional and amateur boxers. He also taught many young people valuable lessons in self-defense, which gave them confidence in many other areas of their lives as well. He acted for many years as a director of Golden Gloves, Deputy Commissioner of Boxing for the state of Minnesota, and inspector for the Minnesota State Athletic Commission. Major Neff was awarded the title of Mr. Boxing for his many contributions to the sport, the award of Upper Midwest Golden Gloves Director of the Year, and the Old Guards of the Ring Award. For his service to the community, he received numerous awards, including an award from the St. Paul Police Force, City of St. Paul Mayor's Certificate of Appreciation, Certificate of Appreciation from the Minnesota Department of Public Welfare, and the Crime Victims Center. Barney Neff died in 1983.

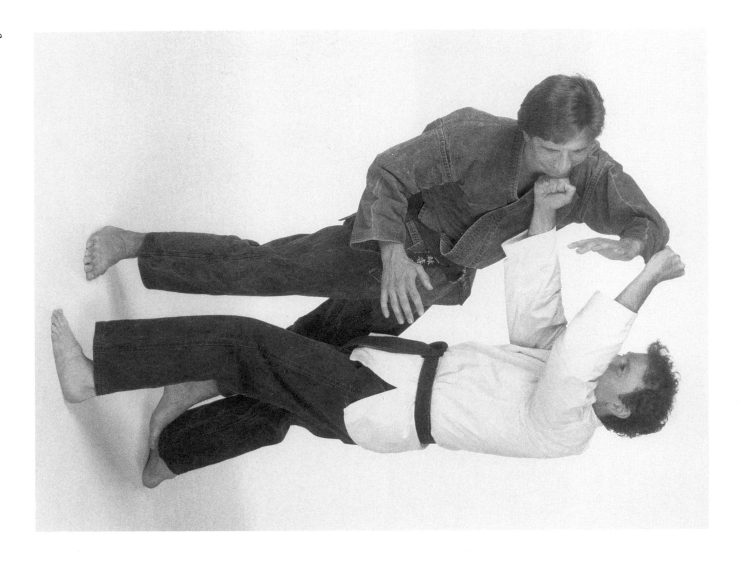

# 1

# INTRODUCTION

Ever since organized warfare began, fighting commandos have engaged in thrilling adventures. A commando is a specially trained soldier—such as a Green Beret, an Israeli paratrooper, a member of the British Special Air Service, or a ninja—who ferrets out secrets of an enemy, takes action behind enemy lines, or uses secret and unconventional fighting techniques. Although legend and historical truth often become blurred in stories about commandos, many of these special fighters have been true heroes—daring, skilled, and persistent.

One of the earliest stories of a commando action is the legend of the Trojan Horse. The ancient Greeks, unable to penetrate the walls of the city of Troy, made a plan to fool the Trojans. The Greeks built a huge statue of a horse, left it on the battlefield outside Troy, and abandoned the battlefield—or so it seemed. The Trojans, thinking that the giant statue was a prize of war, brought it inside the city gates. Later, when the Trojans were off guard, Greek commandos who had hidden inside the horse sprang out and conquered Troy from within the city walls.

Like most commandos, these Greeks had special fighting techniques. Their fighting art, called *pankration,* used punches, kicks, headbutts, chokes, locks, throws, and general

Independent Picture Service

*A model of the Trojan Horse stands near the ruins of the city of Troy.*

*Green Berets rappel down an icy mountain.*

grappling moves. Pankration was so effective that later soldiers copied Greek fighting techniques. Some modern commando tactics are built on the traditions of the ancient Greeks.

The English and French also developed commando tactics to operate behind enemy lines. The English refined methods of punching and movement that are the mainstay of many fist-fighting techniques used by commandos throughout the world. French kicking techniques and military tactics also remain important in the training of commandos. The great French general Napoleon Bonaparte diligently studied commando mil-itary tactics and regularly read an ancient Chinese classic of military science, Sun-Tzu's *The Art of War.*

Since the end of World War II, fighting techniques from various traditions have formed an international pool of commando tactics. Western commandos have combined their own tactics, long-familiar Japanese jujutsu, and other Eastern fighting styles. From the Chinese comes *ch'uan-fa* (meaning "fist way") tactics, often known as *kung fu* (which simply means "learned man"). These techniques include fast and effective hand and foot techniques that can stun or subdue an opponent. From the large islands of Japan, the island of Okinawa, and Korea come powerful blows derived from *karate* and *tae kwon do*. The most dramatic of the commando movements may be the fighting techniques of the ninja—techniques that remained secret until the 1970s.

*Ninja* means "one who steals in"—a spy. These uniquely talented warriors of ancient Japan sold their skills to warring nobles. In order to sneak behind enemy lines, the ninja needed knowledge of practical psychology, the environment, survival, chemistry, weaponry, and self-defense. Over time, various families of ninja developed in Japan, each with its own special skills, practices, and traditions. During Japan's many centuries of civil war, the ninja were hired as commandos for political groups that needed them. Each side in the civil war had its own hired ninja to penetrate enemy lines and ferret out information.

The ninja's secret fighting techniques and military science have only recently begun to

*Ninjas training in a scene from* American Ninja.

Hollywood Book and Poster

*A scene from* Enter the Ninja *shows those ancient fighting commandos in action.*    Hollywood Book and Poster

filter out to the West. Much of the military science of the ninja is contained in a book titled *Sonshi,* which is the Japanese name for a book long studied by Westerners—Sun-Tzu's *The Art of War.*

Modern fighting commandos, drawing from these Eastern and Western traditions, have developed a repertoire of efficient and effective techniques for hand-to-hand combat.

The goal of this book is to explain important commando techniques from these traditions and to show how to apply them in everyday self-defense. Through them, you can develop confidence, better health, and effective fighting skills. This book does not deal with the more dangerous hand-to-hand combat techniques, since they have no practical use in everyday self-defense. Still, some of the techniques taught here could harm someone. Use them prudently and carefully to avoid injury. This book is not meant to be a substitute for an excellent martial-arts instructor. Instead, the book should supplement a program of properly supervised training.

# 2

# COMMON QUESTIONS

**1. If commando techniques are so effective, why haven't I heard of them?**

The term *commando* came into popular use during World War II to refer to special agents, such as the Free French underground and other select fighting groups, who were sent behind enemy lines. Lately, the term *commando* has not been used very much, so you may not have heard it. Still, you have probably heard the specific name of a group of specially trained soldiers or secret agents— the American Green Berets, for example. No matter what such a group is called, special fighters who can infiltrate enemy lines are commandos. You have probably heard of their special abilities, skills, and effectiveness.

**2. Will commando techniques help someone defend against a larger and more powerful aggressor?**

Many commando techniques can give you an edge against an individual whose physical size or abilities exceed yours. A small person with presence of mind, strong spirit, proper timing, flexibility, and effective techniques can overcome a far larger and more powerful opponent.

**3. If *jujutsu* means "gentle art," how can it be used in combat?**

The term *jujutsu* has often been misunderstood. The "gentle" part of the term refers to

the yielding method of response to an attack. Someone who initially yields can counter with the combined forces of the attacker's momentum and the defender's own added power. For example, if you step back and pull a powerful opponent who lunges forward to push, you can use the opponent's own momentum and strength to throw that person off balance. You can then continue pulling

and use your body as a lever to throw him or her to the ground. The harder an opponent pushes on you, the greater the force of that person's eventual fall when you throw him or her.

The ninja's fighting art called *tai-jutsu* (which means "body art") is similar to jujutsu in that it also uses yielding methods of response to win out over an opponent. If yielding techniques worked against the trained warriors who fought the ninja, you can certainly expect them to work on an untrained bully.

## 4. Were the ninja really great commandos?

If the ninja had not been extremely effective as commandos and spies, the Japanese nobility would not have hired them over and over again for hundreds of years. These special Japanese commandos spent years honing a great variety of techniques to overcome skilled opponents in nearly any combat situation. They repeatedly proved their effectiveness in battle.

## 5. Could the ninja really become invisible?

When we hear about "invisibility," we think of a person taking a magic potion and suddenly disappearing. The ninja warriors, however, had a more practical way of becoming invisible to their enemies. They learned to blend in with their environment—to use camouflage. For example, the ninja often wore suits that blended in with their surroundings. If it was dark, a black suit would help them blend easily into the shadows. They learned how to hide under the water and breathe through tubes so that they could not be seen by their opponents.

At other times, in order to gain time to slip

into hiding, a ninja might distract an adversary or temporarily blind him with a bright flash off some reflective material. These clever adaptations to the environment were the ninja way of invisibility. Modern commandos emulate the ninja's methods of becoming invisible to an opponent by adapting to their surroundings.

### 6. What special fighting methods did the ninja use?

While the basic hand-to-hand combat style used by the ninja was often tai-jutsu, each ninja family developed its own approaches to fighting. The ninja also developed great skill in using standard weapons and adapting some common items for use in battle. Some of the weapons they normally used were the *katana* (sword), *tanto* (knife), *nunchaku* (two sticks attached by a cord), *shuriken* (throwing stars), and *naginata* (a curved blade on the end of a long pole). If none of these were available, the ninja made do by turning other objects into weapons.

The ninja have been called "shadow warriors" because they could slip unseen in and out of a place—sometimes by adapting to the environment and at other times by knowing just the right time to move. Ninja were taught how to climb difficult obstacles, to conceal themselves to escape traps, and to cover their tracks so that they seemed to have never been in an area. They used deception and illusion to confuse and distract others, much as a magician does today. This tremendous flexibility separated the ninja from other, more conventional, warriors.

### 7. What do commandos mean when they claim to use "psychological warfare"?

An effective fighter must harness both mind and spirit. When the mind cannot concentrate or the spirit falters, a fighter weakens. Commandos often try to weaken their opponents mentally and emotionally through a process called "psychological warfare." For example, commandos might plant some misleading information to "psych out" an enemy—to create a frightening illusion that will confuse and distract the opponent. Methods of psychological warfare are also effective in everyday confrontations in which your confidence and ability to fight can discourage bullies. Many fights are first won in the mind.

### 8. How can I learn more about modern commando fighting methods?

You can learn about commando fighting techniques by studying under a qualified instructor of combat jujutsu, hand-to-hand commando techniques, kempo, or ninja fighting methods. Before choosing a teacher, find

well-cushioned gloves and your feet are protected with special training shoes or boots. When you practice throwing or grappling, always use a thickly padded mat made specifically for this type of use.

Even with protective equipment, however, beginning students should not actually make contact with one another with punches, strikes, or kicks. A safety mat does not give you an excuse to actually throw a beginning student. Never throw anyone unless that person has developed excellent falling skills.

out what kind of conditioning and physical stamina the teacher expects of his or her students. Even if you think you can handle the physical training, do not start training until your doctor has approved such a program for you. Also, ask yourself whether you are emotionally and mentally ready to handle the stress of practicing hand-to-hand combat.

## 9. What equipment can help me in my commando training?

Your teacher of commando methods may suggest some kind of training equipment that best fits the fighting art you are learning and the teacher's program of instruction. In general, a beginning student should wear safety equipment such as a headguard, a mouthguard, a groin-cup, shinguards, and a pair of knee pads. When sparring with a partner, also make sure that your hands are covered with

All falls, throws, and grappling moves should be practiced under the supervision of a qualified instructor.

To practice blows, use a large punching bag like the kind used in Western boxing. A mirror can also help students observe their own techniques and compare their performance with a teacher's demonstration or the pictures in a guidebook.

Because some equipment can be very expensive, if possible start your instruction in a school that provides equipment for its students. This will let you decide—before you spend a lot of money—whether you want to continue your training long enough to justify the cost of buying your own equipment.

# CHAPTER

# 3

# BASIC PRINCIPLES

To move quickly and efficiently, commandos follow certain basic principles of combat:

1. *Keep presence of mind.* You can meet almost any challenge if your mind remains free of illusion, distraction, and fear. When your mind is free to focus on the challenge at hand, it can automatically move the body into effective action. To achieve this clarity of thought—often called presence of mind—remain calm when threatened, observe what is happening around you, don't let your mind wander, and don't concentrate on the possibility of being harmed.

One technique for keeping your mind free and calm is called "centering." Concentrate momentarily on the center of your body at a point approximately two inches below the navel. Centering has been used by commandos in the Far East for hundreds of years because it so effectively frees the mind from fear and improves overall stability.

2. *Think of the situation as a challenge, not as an insurmountable problem.* A skilled commando looks forward to a challenge as an opportunity to overcome an inner obstacle (such as a negative self-image) or to achieve physical prowess. If you can develop this positive attitude, you can probably succeed despite the rigors of fighting.

3. *Concentrate all of your abilities on meeting the challenge.* Focus on what you are doing and put everything you've got—all of your mind, spirit, and physical strength—into the task at hand. Don't hesitate, but move forward with confidence.

4. *Plan before you act.* Fighting commandos do not simply charge ahead out of anger or pride. Instead, they have a specific objective in mind. Analyze the challenge in front of you and formulate an appropriate strategy. Consider an opponent's sensitive areas, balance, weaknesses, and strengths before attacking. Form a strategy to take advantage of your greatest strengths while exploiting the opponent's greatest weaknesses.

5. *Take advantage of timing.* No matter how powerful a blow is, it will do no good unless it is thrown at the right time. A powerful baseball player can take a magnificent swing, but if the swing isn't timed properly, the batter will miss the ball. The same principle applies to self-defense action. Carefully time your defense or your counterattack. Look for any gaps in your opponent's attack, such as when the attacker is distracted, is catching a breath, or has just finished throwing a punch. If such gaps do not happen on their own, you can make them happen by forcing your opponent to leave an opening for a properly timed attack.

6. *Use maximum strength against an aggressor's weakest point.* The old saying that a chain is only as strong as its weakest link certainly applies to commando training. Even the most powerful opponent will have more than one weakness that can be exploited. Discover these weaknesses, then use them. For example, you can strike one of the naturally sensitive areas of the body (see diagram page 26.) that your opponent leaves open to attack.

7. *Disrupt an opponent's balance.* A bully's aggressive action will usually put him or her off balance during an attack. You should take advantage of this weakness by further off-balancing the attacker. If, for example, an aggressor pushes you hard, simply pull that person in the same direction to continue throwing him or her off balance. If the aggressor pushes you again, pull on that person to further disrupt his or her balance. Watch carefully for moments when an opponent is likely to be off balance, such as when moving forward or when completing a step in any direction. Execute your counterattack at the exact moment the aggressor is off balance and use that person's momentum against him or her.

8. *Make use of your natural weapons.* People generally use only a very small part of their intelligence, energy, and abilities in any endeavor. By increasing your abil-

ity to use your mind, body, and spirit, you can enjoy a great advantage.

Observe a bully carefully. Does he or she rely on one or two favorite techniques that have worked successfully in the past? If so, outsmart him or her by making those techniques hard to use. Is the attacker a lot larger than you? Neutralize the size advantage by pinching the attacker or striking a sensitive area. You can also use a large aggressor's force of attack to put him or her off balance.

Even if your opponent appears to have great skill in a particular type of fighting, you have many natural weapons. Carefully read and practice the techniques taught in this book so that your whole body becomes a defense mechanism to meet the challenge of an attacker.

9. *Be persistent.* In the old story of the tortoise and the hare, the tortoise, by being persistent, won a race against the much faster hare. You too can overcome powerful adversaries if you persist despite hardship or trouble. Focus not on problems but on solutions, and patiently try to make the solutions work. Try to wear your adversary down. A person who is persistent can often win a fight even though he or she may not be as powerful as the opponent.

10. *Adapt to the challenge.* One reason for the ninja's tremendous success as commandos was their flexibility in meeting the demands of a situation. Creatively adapting to challenges in self-defense (and other areas of life) is crucial. In a real fight, don't try to think of all the steps you have learned and then mechanically apply them. By the time you do so, your opponent may have won. Instead, be ready to use creative combinations and move smoothly from one fighting technique to another.

# CHAPTER
# 4

# CONDITIONING AND
# BASIC SENSITIVE AREAS
# OF THE BODY

To successfully apply commando techniques, you need physical strength, flexibility, and endurance. This does not mean you have to have huge muscles or be a model of grace and agility. Even if you are not very large or graceful, you can condition your body properly. To do this, however, you must be patient and persistent. Avoid stretching your muscles too much at any given practice session. Stretching slowly day by day is better than risking injury to your muscles by pushing the conditioning process too fast.

This chapter will outline some basic stretching and conditioning exercises you need in order to start your training. But first, here are some general guidelines:

Hold slow stretches for at least a count of five to get the desired release of tension. Gradually increase your repetitions of each exercise as it becomes easier. Your conditioning program can include some light weightlifting exercises to build your muscle strength, but only under the supervision of a qualified instructor to ensure that you learn proper and safe techniques. Lift weights on alternate days so that your body has a day between sessions to rest and recover.

Endurance exercises are also very important in preparing you for commando training. Running, swimming, bicycling, and brisk walking are all excellent exercises for building cardiovascular health and general endurance. If you have joint problems, such as weak knees, avoid running. Find conditioning exercises that you will enjoy doing for the rest of your life without undue risk of harm to your body.

Before you start any conditioning program, get a full medical checkup and ask your doctor for advice about exercising. Only after you have received your doctor's approval should you start to condition your body for commando training.

## General Neck Conditioners

Stand erect with your feet slightly apart and your arms hanging loosely at your sides. Drop your chin toward your chest. Let your head move gradually downward. Do not force the motion or push your chin any farther than it can comfortably go. Then lift your head to the starting point and repeat the movement two more times.

Next, starting with your head in a normal upright position, turn your head slowly and gently to the right to look over your right shoulder, and then return to the starting position. Repeat two more times and then do a similar set of three turns to your left side.

Look straight ahead, and then lower your head to the right so that your right ear nears your right shoulder. Stretch only as far as you can without discomfort. Return to your starting position and repeat two more times. Then do the same type of movement on your left side three times.

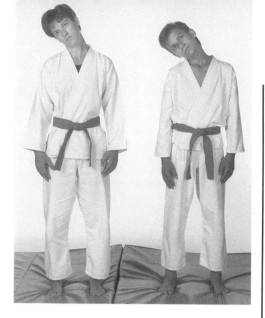

## Basic Back Stretch

Lie with your back flat on an exercise mat, your knees bent, and your feet flat on the mat. Put your hands behind your right knee and bring your leg as close to your chest as possible without straining. Move slowly and gradually. Return to the original position and repeat four more times. Next, do the same exercise five times with your other leg.

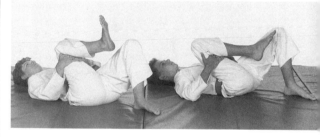

## Basic Sit-up

On an exercise mat, lie with your back flat on the mat, your knees bent, and the bottoms of your feet on the mat. Gently bring your chin up toward your chest. Then slowly sit up as you move your straightened arms toward your knees. DO NOT completely sit up, but let your hands approximately touch your knees. Then slowly return to the starting position. Repeat the exercise five times.

## Toe Touch

Stand erect with your feet slightly apart and your arms hanging loosely at your sides. Your legs should be slightly bent at the knees. Reach both arms above your head and then bend over. Let your arms hang down toward the floor, and stretch. Allow gravity to gradually perform the stretch for you. Your fingers do not have to touch the floor. Don't bounce or force the action; gradually stretch your muscles. Perform this stretch at least five times.

## Basic Side Stretch

Stand erect with your feet apart. Place your left hand on your hip and stretch your right hand up and as far to the left as you can. Straighten up and stretch to the right. Stretch at least three times to each side.

## Body Twist

Stand with your feet apart and your knees slightly bent. Hold your right arm, bent at the elbow, at chest level. Twist at the waist as far to the right as you can comfortably go while stepping back with your right foot. Return to the starting position, raise your left arm to chest level, and do a similar twist at the waist and step to the left. Twist at least three times to each side.

## Basic Back-of-the-Leg Stretch

Place the palms of your hands against another person, a wall, or some other solid object and move your feet back at least three feet away from him, her, or it. Bend your elbows and bring your chest close to the person or object. Hold that position for at least a count of 10.

## Basic Two-Leg Stretch

Stand erect with your feet slightly apart. Slowly spread your legs as far as possible without straining, then return to your starting stance. Perform this stretch only once per exercise session.

## FALLING EXERCISES

Once you start training, you will have to learn how to protect your body when it is thrown to the ground. Practice falling exercises very carefully, only on a safety mat designed for martial-arts use, and only under the supervision of a qualified martial-arts instructor. *Do not allow anyone to throw you, even in practice, until you have developed excellent falling skills, and never throw anyone in practice unless he or she knows how to fall safely.* Also, never practice any throws until your instructor has given you permission and can supervise you.

### Rear Fall

Use this falling technique when you are thrown off balance backward. Begin in a squatting position. Tuck in your chin and extend your arms directly in front of you. Spring up with your knees and allow your body to fall backward. As you fall, extend your arms out to either side of your body. Just before your back hits the mat, slap your forearms down against the mat to break your fall. Your head should not touch the mat at any point during the fall.

## Side Fall

This common falling technique is especially effective when you are thrown over an opponent's hip, shoulder, or leg. Begin in a squatting position with one leg crossed in front of the other. Keep your chin tucked down so that your head never hits the mat. Gradually slide your front leg forward so that you lose balance and fall to your side. While falling, bring the arm on that side up in the air. Just before you hit the mat, slap the palm of your raised hand against the mat to break the fall. Make sure to land without hurting your knees, your ankles, or other sensitive areas.

## Front Fall

The front fall can be effective when someone tackles, sweeps, or throws you forward, or if you slip and fall forward. Start out kneeling on the mat, then begin to stand up, but let your body fall forward. Bring your arms up, with palms facing the mat, and then slap the mat with the palms of both hands to break the fall. Keep your head and abdomen off the mat at all times. Also make sure that your hands and arms remain stationary after they slap the mat so they can support your body and keep it from hitting the mat.

## BASIC SENSITIVE AREAS OF THE BODY

Certain extremely sensitive areas of the human body cannot take much stress or pressure, no matter how well the body is conditioned. Many of the sensitive areas of the body are located on an imaginary line down the middle of the body called the *centerline*. Carefully guard the centerline and all sensitive areas of your body in a confrontation, and look for ways to attack these areas of an opponent's body. A pinch, direct hand pressure, or a sharp blow to a sensitive area of an opponent's body may finish a fight. You may also bend a joint to encourage an opponent to give up.

The two diagrams show sensitive areas of the human body.

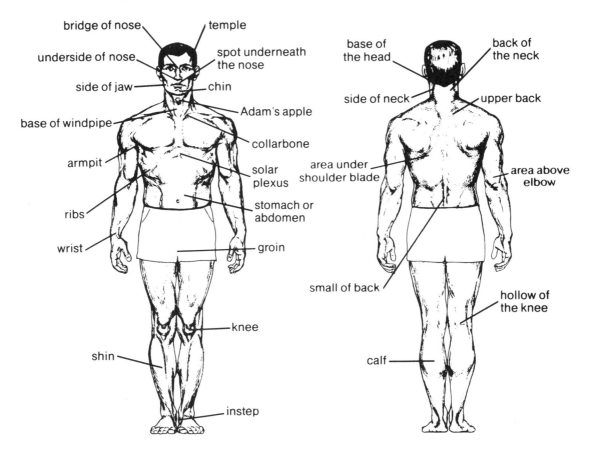

# 5

# STANCES AND MOVEMENT

A strong fighting stance will give you stability and allow you to make defensive moves. In modern commando training, three basic stances work for most combat situations. You may remain in one stance throughout a fight or move from one stance to another to avoid blows and to penetrate an opponent's defenses. Practice these stances repeatedly, and concentrate on learning to assume the basic guard stance as soon as you are threatened. Once you are comfortable with the stances, you can begin some basic movements.

**Natural Stance**

If you are suddenly forced to defend yourself, you will probably start out in a natural stance. This stance is also often used at the start of a throwing technique. The natural stance is comfortable enough to maintain for a long time without tiring. Unless you plan to execute a throw or a hold, however, change to the basic guard stance (explained later) as soon as possible.

To assume the natural stance, stand erect with your feet 6 to 10 inches apart. Keep your shoulders relaxed, your arms hanging comfortably at your sides, your back straight, and your eyes focused directly on your opponent.

To assume a *right* natural stance, begin in

the basic natural stance and simply place your right foot forward. For the *left* natural stance, move your left foot forward from the basic natural stance. In both types of natural stance, keep your upper body facing forward and your weight evenly distributed over your feet.

with your knees deeply bent. Keep your torso erect and your weight evenly distributed over your feet. Besides the basic straddle-leg stance, there are diagonal and side-facing variations. In all varieties of this stance, either hold your hands in fists at your hips or hold both hands open, with palms facing out, at approximately chest level.

## Straddle-Leg Stance

The straddle-leg stance lets you choose different ways of approaching an opponent. It can be used in executing blocks and blows or at the start of a grappling move, and it sometimes serves as a transitional position between the natural stance and the basic guard stance.

To assume a front straddle-leg stance, position your feet 1 1/2 to 2 shoulder widths apart

## Basic Guard Stance

The primary stance for fighting, this stance gives you both stability and mobility. To assume the basic guard stance, stand with your left foot forward and your toes turned slightly inward. Place your right foot a little more than a shoulder width to the back. If you want more stability, put your rear foot flat on the ground. If mobility is more important, rest the ball of your rear foot (the part at the base of the big toe) on the ground and keep your heel about one to two inches off the ground. Make sure that your legs are bent at the knee. Although you should usually distribute most of your weight on the front leg, you might sometimes distribute your weight evenly over your feet. If you are under attack, however, you might want to transfer most of your weight to your rear leg for a short time. Shift back as soon as possible to a basic guard stance with the majority of your weight on the front foot.

Keep your left arm at about chin level with your left hand in a fist or an open-hand position and your shoulders relaxed. Hold your right hand under your ear with the palm facing slightly forward, in either a fist or open-hand position. Keep both elbows close to your sides for protection, and tuck your chin down. Your whole body should feel strong, but loose enough to defend or attack quickly. At the start of a confrontation, try to position your forward foot on a line running between your adversary's feet.

NOTE: The left leg is usually the forward leg for right-handed people. If you are left-handed, you may want to reverse the stance to keep your powerful left hand in the rear. All initial positions shown in this book have the left foot forward unless otherwise specified.

## MOVEMENT

By moving during a fight, you can avoid an opponent's blows, confuse your adversary, and place yourself in a position to execute a maneuver. Try to move in a relaxed manner, and choose moves appropriate to such circumstances as your opponent's size and fighting style, the amount of light present, how much room you have, and the terrain. If you move away from your opponent, move fast enough and far enough to avoid being hit, but stay close enough and stable enough to launch a full-power counterattack. For example, if you evade a punch by jumping too far to one side, you will be unable to strike back at your opponent in his or her moment of weakness just after the punch.

## STEPS

### Short Step

With this step, you can cover a moderate distance quickly and move forward or backward from any stance. To move forward from a basic natural stance, simply step forward and to the side with your front foot into a basic guard stance. Maintain proper balance as you step, and keep your upper body erect.

### Large Step

Use this step to cover a large distance or throw a lot of body momentum into a technique. From the basic guard stance, move your rear leg forward past your front foot so that you assume a basic guard stance with your stepping foot forward.

## Slide Step

This technique allows you to keep the same foot in front of you as you travel. From a basic guard stance, slide your front foot forward. Next, slide your back foot forward until you have regained your original stance. Be sure to maintain proper balance as you move. To go backward, slide your back foot to the rear, and then follow with your front foot.

## Circle Movement

This movement allows you to move around to the opponent's side or back. From the basic guard stance, move your forward foot about eight inches in whichever direction you want to go. Then, pivot on this forward foot as you swing the rest of your body in the desired direction. At the end of this two-step series, you should again be in your stance, but your position in relation to your opponent will be different.

## Side Shift

The side shift is useful in avoiding an aggressor's blows or moving to set that person up for a technique. To side-shift to the left, step in that direction with your left foot and slide your right (rear) foot toward your left until you are once more in a proper stance. A right side shift would involve the same moves but to the other side.

## BASIC DODGES

With an effective dodge, you can evade an aggressor's blow and throw the attacker off balance. Dodging a blow is usually better than blocking it. Dodges are quicker, and even an effective block forces you to absorb force from a blow—which will eventually wear you down. Most well-executed dodges will help you evade an attack and will position you to follow through with a counterattack.

### Pivot Dodge

From a basic guard stance, pivot on your front foot and swing your body away from the aggressor's blow. You should end up slightly off to the side or rear of the attacking limb but still close enough to counterattack. Practice pivoting on the balls of your feet and ending up in a strong stance, ready for action.

## Slip Dodge

In a slip dodge, you move your upper body up or down, side to side, or front to rear, to avoid an attacker's limb. A slip dodge can confuse your opponent and make you a more difficult target. Whether you perform your slip dodge while standing still or while moving, try not to move so fast or so far that you lose stability.

Practice slip dodges only after you have developed a stable basic guard stance and have learned how to step smoothly and quickly with proper balance. Start practicing this dodge by shifting your head and shoulders up and down as if you were evading punches. Next, practice bending your knees deeply as you bend forward at the waist. Then try bending the top half of your body to one side and then to the other. (This side-to-side movement can fake out an opponent.) Then practice bending slightly to the rear from your waist as though to move back from an aggressor's hands. Practice these slip dodging movements from other stances and in combination with the other movements taught in this chapter.

During any upper body movement, focus your eyes on the aggressor, and try to make your slip dodges flow together in an almost continuous motion. You gain a real psychological edge over an adversary if you are difficult to hit but can launch counterattacks from unexpected places.

# CHAPTER

# 6

# DEFENDING AGAINST HAND AND FOOT ATTACKS FROM SAFETY-RANGE AND LONG-RANGE DISTANCES

Evading a blow may not be enough to end a confrontation. Commando training teaches ways to block and counterattack in case evasion is not enough to discourage an attacker.

A single counterattack, however, may not end the fight or even penetrate your opponent's defenses, so additional blows might be needed to weaken an aggressor. A well-matched set of blows or other fighting techniques is called a combination. Each technique in a combination should set up the next one. This chapter will illustrate some combinations used in common self-defense situations.

Practice performing these combinations with proper form, power, and speed, but also be prepared to adapt them to the situations in a real confrontation. Also, combine them with other techniques to create a defense that is timed and adjusted to be effective against a specific opponent.

The effectiveness of your defense, counterattack, takedown, or other techniques will be greatly affected by the distance between you and your opponent. Three major categories of distance between two combatants are important in the fighting arts: safety range, long range, and short range. In safety range, neither combatant can hit the other with his or her longest blow. For example, in safety range, an attacker's side kick will miss you because you are a few inches beyond it. Long range is the distance at which one combatant can hit another with certain lead hand or foot attacks. Techniques such as front kicks, side kicks, or straight punches are usually used at this range. At close range, shorter punching techniques (such as hooks or uppercuts) and grappling techniques can be used.

In practice and in real confrontations, use distance to take advantage of your strengths and your opponent's weaknesses. For example, if your opponent is a better grappler than you are, make that person box from a distance.

Before you can learn to use distance, you must be familiar with the basic movements

that you need in stepping toward, away from, or around an opponent. Practice these movements, and then try executing them with a stationary object as your imaginary opponent. To begin, move straight at the object and then back away. Then, to practice approaching an opponent from an angle, perform a circle movement around the object until you can move smoothly and efficiently to the right or to the left of an opponent. Then practice evading or attacking at an angle by taking a single step off to the side of the opponent, and perform whatever additional movement you feel is necessary. In a real confrontation, you will be able to angle past an aggressor with your body and catch that person by surprise while remaining relatively safe from attacking blows.

Each of the remaining chapters of this book builds upon the foundation you have gained in understanding movement and distancing. If you understand, gauge, and work comfortably within the appropriate distances, you can become a formidable fighter in any physical confrontation.

## CIRCLE DODGE AND COUNTER AGAINST A SIDE KICK

The side-kick technique has a great deal of reach, or ability to cover a lot of distance, and can be used when ordinary front kicks or straight punches will not reach your opponent.

An opponent who turns one side of his or her body toward you might be preparing to throw a side kick. When you see your opponent's front leg begin to bend, take a short step forward to your right side with your left foot and pivot as you swing your rear (right) leg around. Keep your left (front) arm ready to block, if necessary. This circle movement to the right positions your body at an angle to the opponent—out of the way of his or her kicking leg. Once your opponent has thrown the side kick, bring your rear (right) leg off the ground in a bent-knee position and thrust it out to hit that person's body or supporting leg with a powerful front kick. Place your right foot back down and, if necessary, execute a punch on the same side.

## DEFENSE AGAINST A FRONT KICK

The front kick, a very quick lead technique, does not have as great a reach as the side kick, but it can be devastating if it hits you. A front kick can be thrown with the forward or rear leg.

If an aggressor throws a front kick at you, sweep your forward arm down to deflect the attacking leg. Try to turn the aggressor's body to the outside with your block so that the person cannot easily follow up with a punch. Then make your rear hand into a fist and throw a right straight punch. As you hit the attacker, your knuckles should be facing up and your left arm should be ready to block any blows by your opponent. Because the right straight punch is thrown with your rear hand, your body weight helps power it forward. Even so, it should be used only as a follow-up to a block or other lead technique because it is too easily blocked or countered when thrown first.

If your punch does not take all of the fight out of your opponent, you may have to follow up with another blow from your left hand. First, make your left hand into a fist. Then, from its forward position in the basic guard stance, turn the fist a quarter turn as you launch it from the shoulder so that the knuckles will be on top. This punch—the left jab—can also be used as a lead technique because it allows you to close distance on an opponent while forcing him or her to either defend or be hit. A left jab, however, is not a knockout punch and should be used with additional techniques to end a fight.

## DEFENSE AGAINST A ROUNDHOUSE KICK

The roundhouse kick can be used to attack from an angle. It is more commonly thrown using the rear leg. An opponent will often assume an opposite stance, with the right leg forward, and use a left rear roundhouse kick to attack your centerline. When the attacker lifts his or her rear leg and turns it so the knee is off to the side, you should be prepared to defend against the roundhouse kick. This can be done by moving to the rear or to the side, or by a block. If there is limited space, you may be forced to block.

If the kick is aimed at your lower body, intercept the kicking leg below the knee by lowering your right (rear) hand. Protect yourself from a roundhouse kick aimed above the groin but below the head by holding your rear arm up in a bent-arm position with the soft part of the forearm out and the forward arm up similarly across your body. To block these roundhouse kicks move your rear bent arm to intercept the lower part of the attacking limb.

If the attacker attempts an upper-level kick to your head, follow up your block with a takedown. Bring both of your forearms up to block the kick; your forward arm should make contact first to stop the blow. Then slip your rear arm up and around to trap the kicking leg. At the same time, move close to the attacker and slip your closest leg behind the attacker's supporting leg, sweeping it out from underneath him or her.

## DEFENSE AGAINST LEFT JABS

The left jab is a very fast lead technique that can also be used by a skilled aggressor throughout the fight to keep you off balance and confused.

## ALTERNATIVE ONE—DEFENSE AGAINST AN UPPER-LEVEL LEFT JAB WITH PARRY AND COUNTER

If an aggressor throws a left jab at your head, step forward with your left foot as your right hand comes up and sweeps the punching arm outward and away from you. Counter the attack with a one-two punch combination by delivering a left jab followed by a right straight punch—both aimed at the aggressor's head.

## ALTERNATIVE TWO—DEFENSE AGAINST A MID-LEVEL LEFT JAB WITH PARRY AND COUNTER

If an aggressor launches a left jab at your chest, bring your right (rear) hand up to meet the outside of the attacking arm, deflecting it down, in, and away. Then grab the attacker's arm with your right blocking hand. At the same time, snap your left arm out at the elbow so that you hit that person with a backfist strike (the back of your closed fist). Reaching down with your left hand to grab the attacker's left wrist, follow through with a right punch to the aggressor's head.

## ALTERNATIVE THREE—DEFENSE AGAINST AN UPPER-LEVEL LEFT JAB WITH DODGE OUTSIDE AND COUNTER

If an aggressor moves forward while executing a left jab, you may dodge it and still be near enough to counterattack. Drop your weight back to your right leg and quickly turn your left shoulder to the right so that the aggressor's jab moves over that shoulder. To counterattack, while you are turning bring your left arm around with a hooking motion to strike your opponent. On impact, keep the thumb side of your fist facing upward. Keep your right hand held high so you can throw an uppercut to that person's body.

## DUCKING WILD SWINGS

If an aggressor uses a windmill attack—attacking while wildly swinging the arms—avoid harm and quickly counter the attack with a simple ducking dodge. As the aggressor throws the first swinging punch, bend the top part of your torso forward so that the blow swings harmlessly over you. Keep both of your hands high and ready for action. You can counterattack by throwing an uppercut with either arm to your aggressor's stomach, ribs, or solar plexus. Put power into your uppercut by bending your knees before the punch and driving upward with your legs. Follow your first uppercut with another, if necessary.

## DEFENSE AGAINST A RIGHT STRAIGHT PUNCH

If your adversary begins with a right straight punch, you have an indication of your opponent's lack of experience. Such a technique can be easily spotted, and leaves a fighter wide open to a counterattack.

## ALTERNATIVE ONE—OUTSIDE PARRY OF A RIGHT STRAIGHT PUNCH

If an opponent throws a right straight punch, bring your left hand up to parry it from the outside. Using only as much movement as needed, deflect the blow inward, aside, and down. To counterattack, drive your right hand with a straight punch over that person's right limb to his or her head, and, if necessary, follow through with an additional left hand blow.

## ALTERNATIVE TWO—INSIDE PARRY OF A RIGHT STRAIGHT PUNCH

If an opponent throws a right straight punch, use the palm of your left hand to parry it from the inside. Forcefully push the attacking limb out and away. Your right hand should be in a position to defend against any other blows or to counterattack with a right straight punch to the chin. If necessary, follow through with a left punch.

## DEFENSE AGAINST A RIGHT LUNGE PUNCH

Sometimes an aggressor will use a lunge punch—a technique that involves lunging forward and punching from the same side. The lunge adds power and reach to the punch. When an aggressor starts to throw a right lunge punch, perform a side-shift movement to your left from a natural stance, a diagonal straddle-leg stance, or a basic guard stance. With your left hand, parry the right punch from the outside and deflect it inward. Follow with a right straight punch to the aggressor's body. Then grab the aggressor's punching arm with your right hand as you launch a left punch to the side of his or her head. To finish, grab the aggressor's upper right arm with your left hand and grab his or her wrist with your right hand, while you use your left leg to sweep the aggressor's right leg out from under him or her.

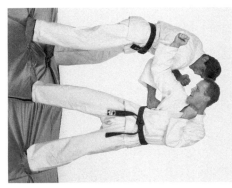

# HANDLING HAND AND FOOT ATTACKS FROM CLOSE RANGE

When a heated argument leads to a physical attack, the aggressor and defender are likely to be at close range. At this range, an aggressor may launch a short punch, an elbow strike, or a knee attack. The defender can respond effectively with short punches such as hooks or uppercuts.

If you find yourself in a close combat situation, you must be careful to stay in this range only if you have the advantage. For example, if your opponent is taller and has a longer reach than you, you can neutralize your opponent's advantage by bringing the fight closer to that person. Tie up a taller opponent's arms so that his or her best punches and kicks cannot be used against you, while your shorter arms work against that person's body. If you are the same height as your opponent, it may be best to enter close range to counterattack, but then move away quickly so that you are outside the hitting range of blows that your aggressor favors.

If you are a good wrestler, you can take advantage of close range and take your adversary to the ground. But if you are taller than your adversary, you will want to avoid being in close range so that you do not lose the benefit of momentum and reach that your longer limbs give you. This chapter introduces basic techniques for defending yourself from close-range blows.

## DEFENSE AGAINST A CLOSE VERTICAL FIST

At close range, an attacker might launch a vertical fist at your head by throwing a punch squarely from his or her forward side. This punch shoots straight out with the thumb side of the fist facing upward. You can defend against such a technique by using a slip dodge and/or parrying the blow outward or inward. Since vertical punches are often thrown by an attacker whose body is turned to face you, they often create opportunities for countering by attacking your opponent's exposed centerline.

## ALTERNATIVE ONE—DEFENSE AGAINST A VERTICAL PUNCH WITH INITIAL INSIDE COUNTERATTACK

If an aggressor throws a vertical punch, evade it by using a slip dodge, but not one that takes you too far to the left or right. Immediately extend the middle knuckle of your right fist and shoot the fist out to hit a sensitive point on the aggressor's body. Next, use upper-body motion to move around to the outside of the aggressor's left arm as you deliver a left hook to the midsection. Finish by crossing your right arm over the aggressor's left with a punch to the head.

nent's midsection. Step forward and to the left with your left foot bringing your body around the aggressor's left arm to an inside position, and execute a powerful right hook punch to the opponent's ribs or midsection. Finish by driving your body upward to a nearly straight position while executing a left uppercut to the aggressor's chin.

## ALTERNATIVE TWO—DEFENSE AGAINST A VERTICAL PUNCH WITH INITIAL OUTSIDE COUNTERATTACK

When an aggressor starts to throw a left vertical fist punch, move outside the path of the blow. Bring the fingers of your open left hand together, placing your thumb against your palm. Snap that hand out in a wide circle so that the thumb side strikes the oppo-

47

## DEFENSE AGAINST A LEFT HOOK

The duck dodge described in the previous chapter can be used to defend against the left hook. Do not, however, attempt to dodge the attack by leaning back to avoid it. Most hooks are too fast and unexpected for you to evade them this way. Another safe way to handle a hook punch is to bring your right hand up to block it.

If an attacker throws a left hook toward your head, bring your right arm up from your basic stance so that the outside of your right forearm meets the inside of the attacker's hook. Counterattack by shooting your right fist out toward the attacker's head. If you want to follow up with your own left hook to his or her head, turn your left hip to the right while bringing your left arm around in a hooking motion. (The thumb side of your fist should be facing upward.)

If the attacker throws a left hook to your body, simply block the blow with your right elbow and counter with a short right straight punch to his or her head.

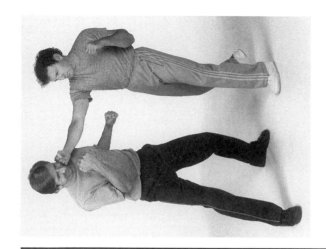

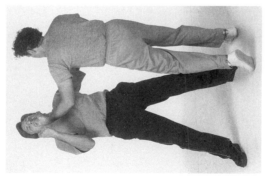

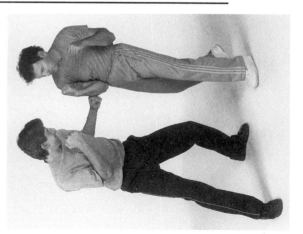

## DEFENSE AGAINST A RIGHT UPPER-CUT TO CHIN OR SOLAR PLEXUS

You can counter an uppercut from either of the aggressor's hands with a parrying action. When the aggressor throws a right uppercut to your solar plexus, bring your right hand down to meet the attacking hand or wrist. Make sure to deflect the blow down and away from your body. You may counterattack with a left hook to the aggressor's head. Unless you move quickly, however, the aggressor may follow up with a left hook to your head.

If the aggressor throws a left uppercut, parry it with your left hand. Counterattack with a right straight punch to the chin followed by a left uppercut of your own.

## DEFENSE AGAINST ELBOW ATTACKS FROM CLOSE RANGE

Elbow attacks can be very difficult to defend against because they come quickly and at odd angles. Nonetheless, you can parry them by pushing the palm of your hand out to meet the attacking elbow and to deflect it outward. Counterattack with an uppercut to the aggressor's body.

## DEFENSE AGAINST A KNEE ATTACK

A simple knee attack directed at the groin or lower stomach is one of the more common and painful close-range attacks. Avoid it either by pushing your palm down to intercept the knee or by turning so that the knee strikes the side of your thigh and not your groin.

## DEFENSE AGAINST A CLOSE KICK

If an aggressor begins to execute a front kick from very close range, neutralize it with a kick of your own. Bend and raise your closer leg, and then drive your leg out to check the aggressor's leg.

## DEFENSE AGAINST A RUSHING ATTACK

Aggressors who rush forward to deliver short close-range punches sometimes leave the vulnerable centerline of the body unprotected. Take advantage of the aggressor's vulnerability by quickly moving forward with a strong set of blows. Keeping your hands up for protection, place your head on the aggressor's chest and press forward to deliver alternate uppercuts to his or her stomach. This should cause the aggressor to lose balance and fall back on his or her heels. Then reach down with both hands and pull the aggressor's legs out from underneath so that he or she is thrown backward.

If the aggressor tries to hit you, punch inside the attacking limb to keep the blow away. You will, in effect, be executing both a block and a punch. Should the aggressor get past your guard, you may neutralize the attack by grabbing him or her in a clinch.

## USING THE CLINCH AGAINST CLOSE-RANGE ATTACKS

When you are in close range during a confrontation, use a clinch hold to tie up your opponent's hands. If you can break the rhythm of repeated hand attacks, you will have a chance to compose yourself or to get a proper grip in preparation for grappling. You can also use a clinch to hold an opponent while you follow through with hand attacks of your own.

Make sure that you are in close range before attempting a clinch. Put your hands on the opponent's shoulders, then quickly move them down your opponent's arms so that your hands grasp his or her biceps. If necessary, pull one of the opponent's arms under your armpit to lock it tighter into position.

Even though your opponent is restricted in a clinch, he or she is not powerless. Keep your head tucked in so your opponent cannot easily hit you. Watch out for a crouching opponent, who may try to move suddenly upward and perform a shoulder- or head-butt. If the adversary moves to break away and punch, tip him or her off balance with a swaying action of your arms and body.

Once you have neutralized the opponent's aggressive hand techniques, you can shift one of your hands to grip the front of his or her shirt or shoulder while the other hand reaches back behind that person's elbow on the other side. This move can work well as a prelude to takedowns and throwing actions.

To release your opponent from a clinch—without making yourself a close and easy target—position your right hand behind the opponent's left elbow and your left hand behind his or her left shoulder. With your right, pull the opponent's arm away to your left while your left hand pushes in the same direction to spin the opponent's body away off balance. When you break a clinch, keep your hands ready to block until you are out of range of the attacker's blows. It is sometimes effective to deliver a left jab to your opponent while moving away from a clinch.

# CHAPTER
# 8

# HANDLING PROLONGED FIGHTING SITUATIONS

Sometimes, a few basic self-defense techniques can quickly end a confrontation. At other times, however, a prolonged fight is unavoidable. You must be prepared to deal with this type of long, intense battle. Proper training can provide you with the fist-fighting and/or grappling techniques you will need in a prolonged fight.

When you first face an attacker, do not try to guess whether this confrontation will turn into a prolonged fight. Simply use whatever basic self-defense move appears to be appropriate to end the fight. If this doesn't take the fight out of your opponent, try something else.

The old saying, "The best defense is a good offense," applies at this stage of a fight. Unless you act assertively, you might get worn out by the power of an opponent's repeated blows or by the motions you make to evade his or her attacks. When you seize the psychological edge by launching your own attacks, however, you can turn the tide of a prolonged fight in your favor.

The basic blows introduced earlier as defensive counterattacks can also form an effective offense, especially if you combine them wisely. One blow may not stop an ad-

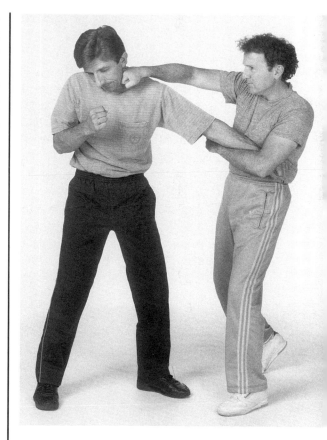

versary, but a series of well-executed techniques might. Practice individual techniques, and after you have become comfortable with them, try using them together in smooth patterns. Concentrate on coordinating foot, hand, and body movements for a smooth technique. Do not continually repeat the same combination of techniques in a real fight. If your moves are predictable, an adversary will soon figure out how to penetrate your defenses. Also, watch your opponent's moves so that you can adjust your tactics. Your combinations should either cause an adversary to leave an area of his or her body open to a defensive technique or wear down that person so he or she gives up fighting.

A combination of techniques should have a rhythm and natural flow. For example, it is natural to lead with your forward left jab and follow up with a straight right. It is also natural to lead with a fast straight punch and then follow up with a hook punch. A good fighter will confuse an opponent by varying the level and angle of attacks. For example, if you mix high punches with mid-level punches—or punches to the right side with blows to the left side—your opponent will have trouble guessing from where the next punch will come. When you want to move into close range, use a combination with a strong lead technique that allows you to advance quickly. As your adversary tries to respond to it, he or she might leave a sensitive body area open to a hit from your next technique. You might even force your opponent into a weaker fighting stance from which you can easily throw him or her off balance. You can then move in to apply a lock or takedown.

Effective combinations allow you to respond naturally to openings in an opponent's defenses or to create openings. Do not just mechanically throw combinations of techniques. Focus on what is happening in a confrontation and use appropriate combinations.

## LEFT JAB/RIGHT STRAIGHT PUNCH/LEFT HOOK

Combining a left jab and a right straight punch can be very effective, especially when you follow up with an unexpected left hook. As an attacker moves forward, lead with a left jab. If the jab is blocked or is not enough to stop the fight, bring your arm back into position and drive your right hip forward while delivering a right straight punch. Finish by taking a short step to the right with your rear foot while suddenly twisting your left hip forward and bringing your left hooked arm around (with the thumb side of the hand facing up) to strike your opponent's head. This three-way combination works effectively from one side of the body to the other to build power.

## LEFT JAB/LEFT JAB/RIGHT STRAIGHT PUNCH

Keep the opponent at a distance with a couple of quick left jabs. Then follow through with a powerful right straight punch to a sensitive area.

## LEFT JAB/LEFT HOOK/ RIGHT UPPERCUT

If your opponent is very skilled at blocking long-range punches, try to get closer by leading with a left jab. Then move forward as you quickly bring your left arm to a coiled position and execute a left hook from close range. Follow through with a right uppercut.

## RIGHT UPPERCUT/LEFT HOOK/
## RIGHT STRAIGHT PUNCH/
## RIGHT KNEE

If you are close to an opponent who leaves an opening to the stomach or solar plexus, drive a right uppercut toward it. After contact, recoil your right arm as you throw a left hook to the side of his or her head. If the opponent continues the fight and moves to regroup, follow up with a right straight punch to the head. If necessary, move closer and drive your right knee up into your opponent's groin or stomach.

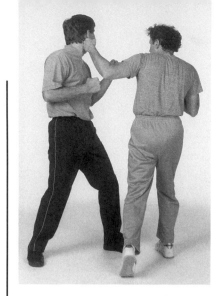

## FRONT KICK/LEFT JAB/ RIGHT STRAIGHT PUNCH

This combination is a good way of advancing on an adversary. First slide your rear (right) leg forward as your front (left) leg lifts off the ground and coils. Snap your left foot out hard and strike your opponent's knee or groin with the ball of your foot. Immediately step back down with your left foot and follow up with a left jab and then a right straight punch.

## RIGHT UPPERCUT/RIGHT HOOK/ LEFT UPPERCUT OR LEFT JAB

If you are close to an aggressor, you can start an effective combination by driving a right uppercut into his or her solar plexus. Immediately follow up by bringing your right arm back into a coiled position and shooting a right hook punch to the jaw. If your opponent bends forward, drive your left arm out with an uppercut to the chin; if he or she moves backward, use a left jab (a long-range blow) instead of the uppercut.

## LEFT JAB/RIGHT STRAIGHT PUNCH/ RIGHT FRONT KICK

If your adversary is good at moving in and out to avoid your counterattacks, use combinations that quickly cover a long distance. A simple combination of left jab, right straight punch, and right front kick should work. The kick should give you a reach long enough to hit an adversary moving backward after the first two blows.

# CHAPTER
# 9

# BASIC GRAPPLING
# MANEUVERS

An adversary who prefers using wrestling maneuvers will attempt to close distance and grab hold of you. Depending on your own fighting skills, you may decide to grapple. This chapter first presents some simple grappling techniques that you can use by themselves or in combination with each other. Later in the chapter, you'll learn about some more complicated techniques to use in a prolonged confrontation. All of these grappling techniques are especially effective against an opponent who is uncomfortable with close-range fighting.

The clinching action is the bridge between fist-fighting and grappling. Once you have decided to move from the clinch to grappling, make all your moves crisply and with full effort. Keep your stance stable and control your momentum; otherwise, your opponent will be able to put you off balance and use your weight against you. Also, make your moves quickly to keep your opponent from landing kicks on your knees or shins. If your opponent is good at throwing strong punches, try to move behind him or her to avoid those blows and to execute an effective takedown.

You might choose to apply a hold if you think you could easily get your opponent into one. In a real fight, you have to move quickly to apply any holds. In practice sessions, however, do them slowly, emphasizing proper form over speed and being very careful not to injure your partner.

In an actual confrontation, you can escape from an opponent's hold by taking advantage of the aggressor's force and momentum. Instead of resisting it, redirect it. If your opponent pushes you, pull him or her in the same direction. If your opponent pulls you, push him or her. Use arm, leg, and hip action to add power to your redirection of this force, and be persistent. If one escape attempt fails, try other movements until you succeed.

If you can't neutralize a hold or a grappling attack by escaping or even counterattacking, you may have to take offensive action. Blend your movements to flow together without any awkward delays that might give your opponent time to respond.

Act confidently and decisively. Once you move to apply a hold in a real fight, do not stop halfway for fear of counterattack. If the hold cannot be applied, move into a clinch immediately. Beware, however, of using the clinch against a far stronger opponent. Against a stronger opponent, use a clinch only briefly to stop a hand attack. Then, as soon as possible, break the clinch and move away.

## ESCAPE FROM AN AGGRESSOR'S GRIP

Sometimes you can escape from an aggressor's grip by simply pinching that person or bending his or her thumb, fingers, or wrist.

## ESCAPE FROM A TWO-HANDED CHOKE

If the aggressor begins to choke you from the front, reach up and grab the small fingers of that person's hand. Bend them outward to release the grip. As long as you hold his or her fingers, you are in control.

## ESCAPE FROM A POWERHOUSE HAND GRIP

Whether you are standing or on the ground, you can push an opponent's thumb back or bend it to escape from his or her grip. If an opponent grabs your hand from the front, simply bring your fingers around his or her thumb and apply pressure to force the thumb back and down, inflicting enough pain to force him or her to release the grip.

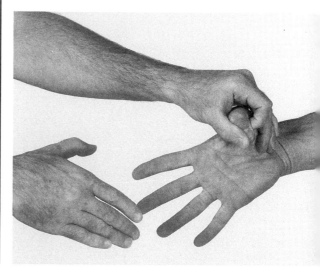

## WRISTLOCK AGAINST A GRABBING ATTACK

Intercept an aggressor's grabbing arm by bringing your closer arm up to meet and stop it. Then grasp the aggressor's grabbing arm with both of your hands. Bring the captured hand around so that its palm faces the aggressor and the thumbs of your hands have a grip on it. Step forward to place your (right) leg behind the aggressor's closer leg and continue to apply pressure as you twist the captured hand outward and away from his or her body. If necessary, follow up by using your right leg to sweep the aggressor's leg out from underneath him or her.

## SINGLE-ARM LEVER AGAINST A POWERFUL GRAB

When an adversary reaches out to grab you, bring your hand up to parry the attacking limb. Then grab that person's wrist with the parrying hand. Bring the opponent's arm out and around so the elbow is facing up, while you turn your body to face the same direction as the opponent. Place your other hand firmly on the back of the captured arm by the elbow. Turn your opponent's wrist until the palm faces up, and push down with your other hand on the attacker's elbow. Then bend the hand of the captured arm back and apply pressure. If this arm bar/wristlock combination does not stop the attack, place one of your legs firmly in front of the opponent and sweep back against the leg closest to you.

## RELEASE FROM A NECK GRIP

When an opponent facing you places a right hand behind your neck to force you downward, immediately push the gripping arm up and out with your left hand while ducking your head down and around to escape. As your head begins to move back upward, grab the aggressor's right wrist with your right hand and his or her upper right arm with your left hand while you drive your knee up into his or her stomach or groin. If necessary, finish by throwing your opponent. To do this, bring your attacking leg down and around as you pivot on your stationary leg. Bring the back of your right leg up tightly against the aggressor's right leg and push the opponent backward while sweeping the leg out so that he or she falls to the ground.

68

## ESCAPE AND THROW WHEN BEING PUSHED BACKWARD

You can execute a throw to defend against an attacker who bears down on you in a clinch or pushes you backward. Reach up with your right hand and grab the front of the opponent's shirt while your left hand tightly holds his or her right arm. Continue pulling your opponent in the direction of the force that is being applied against you, and step forward with your right foot. Pivot on that foot, swing your left leg around, and shift your right hand from your opponent's shirt to his or her waist. Pull down on your opponent's right arm with your left hand as you bend your knees and start to bring the aggressor's body across your right hip. Spring up from your bent-knee position as you execute a hip throw.

69

## ESCAPE AND THROW WHEN BEING PULLED FORWARD

If an aggressor pulls you forward or attempts a clinch, you can use your closeness and your opponent's momentum to your advantage. Pull up on the front of the opponent's shirt and grab his or her right arm with your left hand as you press forward with your right shoulder. At the same time, bring your right leg forward and sweep the aggressor's right leg out so that he or she falls to the ground.

## HANDLING A CHARGING ATTACK

When an aggressor charges forward to grab or strike, move to finish the confrontation with a throw. First, flick your right hand out toward that person's face as a distraction, and then immediately move forward to place your head alongside the aggressor's right hip. Drive your body forward, grab the aggressor's legs, and then pull both of his or her legs toward you. Try to avoid a potential kick by the grounded aggressor.

## RELEASE FROM A HAMMERLOCK

When an opponent moves behind you and grabs one of your arms to apply a hammerlock, step forward with the leg on the opposite side from the arm being held. Bend your body forward at the waist in order to straighten the arm that is being held. Turn your body at the waist as you stand up so that you begin to face the aggressor. Drive a front kick with your rear leg to his or her knee or groin and pull your captured arm out and away. Then resume a basic guard stance.

71

## ESCAPE FROM REAR STRANGLEHOLD

A rear stranglehold is one of the most dangerous holds that an aggressor can apply, but you can break it by moving quickly before your opponent can bend your body backward. As you feel one of the aggressor's hands pushing down on your head and the other circling your neck, reach up and grab the hand that is behind your head. Pull back, if necessary, on one of your opponent's fingers to release the grip as you bring his or her arm up and then forward over your head and across your shoulder with the palm of the hand facing upward. Next, grab the aggressor's arm with your other hand as you pull downward to apply pressure against the back of the elbow. You should now have that person locked in a straight-arm hold that can prevent further aggression.

## ESCAPE FROM A TWO-HAND PRESS ON THE SHOULDERS

A takedown can be effective in stopping an aggressor who bears down on your shoulders with both hands. First try to escape and position yourself behind the aggressor so that you will be safe from hand attacks. Quickly push one of the opponent's elbows upward as you swing around behind him or her. Then grab the opponent. Push out against the back of the aggressor's upper leg or knee with your leg, as you throw him or her backward to the ground.

## ESCAPE FROM AN OPPONENT'S ATTEMPT TO THROW

An opponent who is skilled at throwing techniques will have learned through practice how to grab one of your arms and position his or her back in front of you to throw you over his or her hip or shoulder. In this predicament, immediately relax and try to center your mind. At the same time, place your free hand on the opponent's lower back and drive your knee, on the opposite side from the arm that is being held, up and into that person's posterior to push him or her off balance to the front. Then make a fist with your free hand and, extending your middle knuckle, drive it deeply into the area just above the opponent's hip. This combined action should force the opponent to stop attempting to throw you.

## STRAIGHT-ARM BAR FROM A CLINCH

If an aggressor puts you in a clinch and keeps one of his or her arms almost straight, you may be unable to punch or perform a takedown. However, you can still apply a straight-arm lock. Swing your right hand and forearm around the aggressor's upper left arm, and trap his or her lower left arm against your right side. Press your left hand against the top of the aggressor's left shoulder while your right hand holds tightly to his or her lower left arm. Press forward against the left shoulder with the palm of your left hand while you bring your lower right arm upward against the back of your opponent's elbow. For added force, lean slightly backward as you press against your opponent's left shoulder.

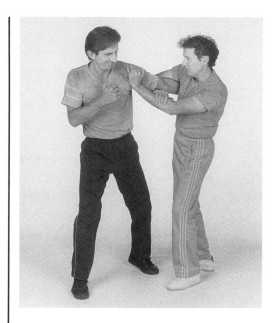

## ESCAPE FROM A GRABBING ACTION

When an opponent grabs you from the front, apply pressure to key spots on his or her body. (See the diagrams on page 26.) Learn the many vulnerable spots of the body so you can attack them whenever they are left open in a confrontation.

## ALTERNATIVE ONE—ESCAPE FROM GRIP BY PRESSURE ON UPPER LIP

With whichever hand can most easily reach your opponent's face, grab his or her upper lip between your thumb and forefinger.

## ALTERNATIVE TWO—ESCAPE FROM GRIP BY PRESSURE ON NECK

Drive your thumbs upward into the attacker's neck on both sides of his or her chin and apply pressure until the aggressor backs away.

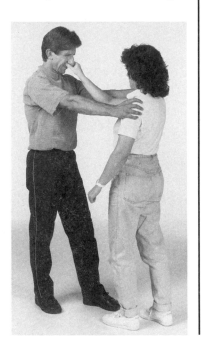

# 10

# DEFENSES FROM THE GROUND

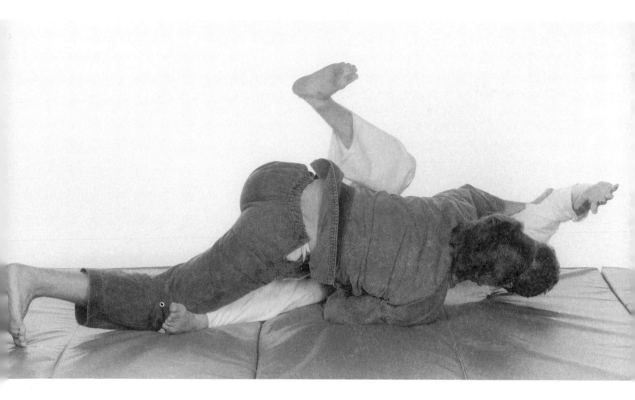

If you are forced to fight while you are on the ground, take charge of the situation by quickly going on the offensive. (Because counterattacks from the ground are very difficult, the combatant who is on offense has a great advantage.) If you do successfully end up on top, move quickly to bring the aggressor's body down flat against the ground so that he or she is unable to get at you with further blows. Do this by knocking out or locking in one of your opponent's arms or legs. Without the support of one of these limbs, your opponent can easily be forced to the ground at the unsupported corner, much like a table that has lost a leg. If your adversary is weak at one limb, attack there, but do it quickly. Also make sure that you keep your own weight distribution balanced on all four corners. If you put too much of your weight on your head and shoulders, your adversary will be able to pull you forward onto the ground.

Even if you end up on the bottom, take the offensive. Your opponent, who has the advantage of weight distribution, will try to pin you down. If you keep moving unpredictably, however, the changes in the direction of your momentum can force your opponent to waste a lot of effort adjusting to your moves. Keep looking for a chance to escape. One way to create an opportunity is to push against the thumb of the opponent's gripping hand so that he or she releases the hold. Then move into a position in which you have enough leverage to bring your opponent to the ground or to execute a blow. Your goal is to put enough distance between you and the aggressor so that you can resume a confident defense from the basic guard stance.

## TAKEDOWN FROM THE GROUND AGAINST A STANDING AGGRESSOR

If you are on the ground facing a standing aggressor who is advancing upon you, propel the left side of your body forward with a rolling action. When your left side hits your attacker's forward leg, begin to wrap your left arm around the outside of his or her ankle. Continue turning your body with a roll as you pull the aggressor's leg forward, forcing him or her to fall backward. Once both of you are on the ground, follow through with an elbow strike and additional blows, if necessary.

## ESCAPE FROM A PIN

If an adversary is on top of you and pins your arms to the ground, escape by moving your arms straight up as you force your hips upward to throw the aggressor forward. Then twist your body to the side and throw the aggressor off.

## ESCAPE FROM A FRONT CHOKE

If an aggressor bears down on you with a choke while your back is on the ground, grab his or her wrists to pull them away. While the aggressor is distracted by your wristhold, bend both of your knees so they are slightly off to the side. Bring your knees up near the front of your body and thrust your legs up and out so that your heels strike the aggressor's ribs. Continue pushing with your legs until you force the aggressor away.

## ESCAPE AND COUNTER FROM A CHOKE FROM THE SIDE

If an adversary has you on your back and begins to choke you from the side, release the pressure by grabbing hold of his or her little fingers. Lift them up and outward and twist your body off to the side, throwing your adversary backward to the ground. (During practice, be very careful not to use force on your practice partner's fingers.) To end the fight, follow through with a series of blows to sensitive areas of the aggressor's body.

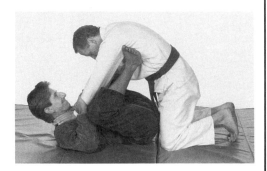

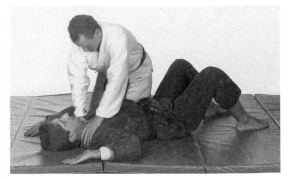

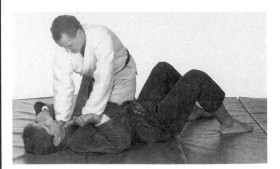

## HANDLING A REAR CHOKE

When you are on the ground and being choked from the rear, grab both of the aggressor's wrists. At the same time, bring your bent legs up and thrust them out at the aggressor to force a release of the hold.

## ESCAPE WHEN AN AGGRESSOR'S HANDS PRESS YOUR SHOULDERS TO THE GROUND

When an aggressor is positioned between your legs and pins your shoulders to the ground, grab one of his or her wrists with both of your hands. Next, raise up your bent leg on the same side as the aggressor's captured wrist and hook it over the elbow of that arm. Twist the aggressor's wrist until the palm of his or her hand faces up. Push down hard with your bent leg on the aggressor's elbow to throw him or her over and down. Turn your body to the side and continue applying pressure against the aggressor's locked elbow while you press his or her hand back at the wrist. You should end up facing to the side with your opponent face-down in a combination straight-arm bar and wristlock.

out to the side, pressing your feet against the ground for stability. Then, slide one of your arms around the opponent's head and turn that person's head to the side as you start to move behind him or her. Once you are behind your opponent, keep one of your arms under your opponent's arm so that your hand rests against his or her neck. If necessary, push back on your opponent's head. (During practice, be careful not to put any real pressure on your partner's neck.) Finally, rest your body weight on your opponent, intertwine your legs with that person's, and hold this leglock until he or she submits.

## DEFENSE AGAINST A DOUBLE GRIP WHILE KNEELING

### Alternative One

If you and your adversary are kneeling on the ground facing one another, try to break your opponent's balance by pushing backward. When he or she counters by pushing against you, pull forward to bring his or her body down in front of you. Spread your legs

## HANDLING AN ADVERSARY WHEN YOU ARE SIDE BY SIDE

If you and your adversary are side by side with both of your knees and hands on the ground, reach your arm around the adversary's waist and grab his or her closest arm. Rest the top of your head against the opponent's armpit and, pushing forward, pull his or her captured arm backward to force him or her face-first to the ground. Then turn the captive arm palm up and continue pulling on the wrist as you push down on the inside of the opponent's arm near the elbow. Finish by swinging the arm up into a bent-arm bar position, usually called a hammerlock.

### Alternative Two

Once you have moved behind your opponent, grab one of his or her arms and bring it back behind him or her in a hammerlock.

## HANDLING AN AGGRESSOR WHEN YOU ARE BEHIND

If you end up on the ground behind an aggressor, promptly move to force him or her down to the ground. With your left arm, grab the aggressor's left wrist. At the same time, reach under and grab his or her right ankle with your right hand. Lift the aggressor's ankle as you bring your body weight down, and pull the captured leg back and underneath, forcing him or her to the ground. Lock the aggressor's legs into position under you while you pull down and back on the ankle. (Because joints are very sensitive areas of the body, you should never push down on them with any force during practice.)

## ESCAPE WHEN YOU ARE UNDERNEATH AN AGGRESSOR

When you are on your knees and the aggressor is on top of you, begin to escape by grabbing his or her right arm (which is probably holding your body) as you bring your right knee to the left and tuck your head down so that your body is almost in the shape of a ball. Pull the aggressor's right arm down and across and turn your whole body to throw him or her off your hip. Your downed opponent should be lying face-up on the ground, so you can rest one of your knees against him or her and deliver a series of finishing blows.

## ESCAPE FROM A REAR ATTACK—ON THE GROUND TO STANDING POSITION

If an aggressor grabs you from behind when you are on the ground, bring first one leg and then the other up to a bent position. Using your whole body, spring into a standing position and push off your attacker's grip. If the aggressor's arms are still on or near your body once you are standing, pull them away as you pivot and face him or her. Be careful to prevent the aggressor from tackling you while you perform this maneuver.

## HANDLING A GROUNDED ADVERSARY WHO ATTEMPTS TO PULL YOU DOWN

When an adversary on the ground attempts to pull you down, lower your hips, stick out your chest, and pull backward. Use all of the strength of your upper body while pulling with your arms. Back away and to the side if possible. Once free, move away quickly and be prepared to defend against a possible kick.

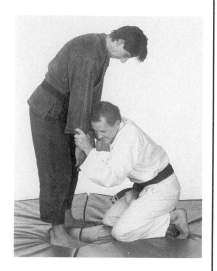

# 11

# STRATEGY

Just as a commando follows a battle plan, you should develop a strategy—a blueprint for successful action. Parts of your strategy can be developed in advance, but be prepared to adjust your plan as a fight progresses. Here are some basic principles for developing a winning strategy.

## MENTAL ATTITUDE

Assume a positive attitude when dealing with an adversary. Do not allow yourself to be intimidated or discouraged. If your opponent tries to gain a psychological edge by threatening you, ignore the threats and concentrate on how you can exploit his or her weaknesses.

## UNDERSTANDING YOUR ADVERSARY

Observe your adversary and try to understand, gauge, and prepare to deal with his or her fighting techniques. Take note of any obvious patterns of action. For example, if your opponent repeatedly stops fighting to verbally taunt you, exploit the opportunity by taking action during that time. If you consciously try to understand the adversary that you are up against, you will be able to take advantage of his or her weaknesses.

## CONTROL THE SITUATION

As soon as possible, take control of a confrontation. If a fight seems likely, take a strong stance and show that you are ready for it. (Your confidence might even discourage a bully and make fighting unnecessary.) If a fight is unavoidable, make sure that it becomes your kind of fight, not your opponent's. Size up the location and how it will affect your ability to move. Never turn your back on an opponent. Keep your eyes on your opponent, and try to see whether he or she has a weapon within reach. An aggressor's eyes and chest movement will often indicate that the body is tensing for an attack. An experienced fighter, however, is capable of a surprise attack unsignaled by any telltale signs.

Don't try to take off your coat or adjust your clothes; if your hands are busy doing that, you are inviting your opponent to attack. Stay alert, and build an overall battle plan to take advantage of your strengths.

## DISTANCE CONSIDERATIONS

Distance is one of the key considerations in self-defense. Never allow your adversary to taunt or force you into fighting his or her kind of fight.

Whenever possible, work from within the fighting range that is most comfortable for you, and try to make your adversary fight from a range he or she finds uncomfortable. For example, if your opponent is a grappler, make him or her fight from a long distance.

Stay out of your opponent's most comfortable range, unless you are at an angle and can hit quickly and move away before he or she can attack you. Leave enough distance between you and an aggressor so that he or she cannot launch a sneak attack with a sucker punch or some other blow while you are off guard.

## ADJUSTING TO THE PARTICULAR SITUATION

Sometimes, a determined, confident look will discourage an adversary. At other times, a simple self-defense maneuver—such as bending back a thumb or applying a wrist-lock—may be enough.

In some cases, however, you will have to go beyond basic self-defense. It is your responsibility to end the fight as quickly as possible, but you should not waste time or energy worrying about how the fight started or whether you missed an opportunity to stop it. Instead, try to defend yourself in whatever way best suits the situation. Follow each blow with others in appropriate combinations. For example, hand and foot combinations tend to confuse an opponent and keep him or her off balance while increasing the likelihood of your winning. Hit your opponent at different heights and from different angles. If your adversary appears to have a weak spot, distract him or her by attacking the face or some other sensitive area and then throw a blow to the weak spot.

Unless you are sure that you are stronger or a better grappler than your opponent, do not try to end a fight by moving into very close range. Also, don't waste your energy by throwing random punches without any clear opening.

## EFFICIENTLY COMBINING DEFENSIVE AND OFFENSIVE TACTICS

Defensive strategies are important, but in a long fight they work best when combined with an effective offense. If you rely exclusively on your ability to evade or block and then counterattack, you are letting an aggressor know that you lack the determination to move forward on your own. You also give your adversary plenty of opportunity to evaluate your defense and eventually penetrate it. If you take the offensive, however, an aggressor will be thrown off balance, and you will be able to control the nature of the fight.

To set the stage for an effective defense, try surprising an aggressor with a straight-line attack at the very start of a fight. Push off your rear leg while keeping your body level, low, and loose, in a fighting stance that will keep you stable and mobile. Use a straight lead technique to get closer to your opponent, not only hitting him or her, but also creating openings for further blows by you. Follow up with explosive hand and foot combinations directed at sensitive areas on the opponent, and try to be unpredictable.

If an opponent throws a punch at you, attack before the aggressor's blow can reach you. For example, if the opponent throws a wild swing or hook punch, throw out a straight punch that will hit him or her first. After throwing your blow, you should be ready to evade, parry, or block a punch. Another tactic is to parry the opponent's blow and then counterattack with the same hand—a technique with which you can move very quickly to surprise your opponent and seize a psychological edge. A more common type of counterattack is a block or parry with one hand and a counterattack from the other side of the body. Time your blows to hit when your opponent is open, off balance, or has exhaled. The efficient use of these tactics may bring the fight to a speedy conclusion.

## TAKING ADVANTAGE OF A WEAKNESS IN THE OPPONENT'S BALANCE

Take advantage of the many times in a fight when your opponent's balance is weak. A fighter loses some balance when changing position to advance or retreat, or when he or she stumbles, or has his or her feet too close together. Watch for these opportunities and use them to your advantage.

## HANDLING DIFFERENT BODY TYPES

When forming a strategy, take into account how your size and physical power compare with your adversary's. Because every adversary will have different strengths and weaknesses depending on his or her height, weight, strength, and experience, you must be able to adjust your strategy accordingly. Your general strategy is to use a decisive technique that forces an adversary to quit.

### Taller and More Powerful Attacker

A taller opponent, who has the advantage of longer limbs, can reach you even while standing beyond the range of your blows. Being smaller, you will most likely have the advantage of speed. Neutralize the opponent's reach by moving in close so that he or she will not be able to gain full hitting power from those long limbs. At close range, you may be able to hit harder, faster, and more often than your opponent. After completing some combination of techniques against your taller and more powerful opponent, withdraw and resume circling him or her from a distance.

In defending, use evasions or parrying actions instead of blocks so that you won't be weakened by blocking—and absorbing—the more powerful blows of your opponent. Defend and counterattack at the same time by evading or parrying while striking with your own counterattack. Set up the opponent by encouraging him or her to throw long lead punches, such as jabs, that will leave an opening for counterattack. As soon as you see a long lead coming, slip in and hit hard with a series of combination blows, and then move away. Do not stay in close range after punch-

ing, unless you know your opponent is off balance.

Be careful that your opponent does not force you into a corner where he or she can deliver a series of fast punches and kicks from a distance. Avoid being in the direct line of an opponent's blows by using circular and angular movements, and be particularly aware of any action the opponent takes to move in at an angle to cut off your mobility. If an opponent grabs you in a clinch, you should not attempt to use strength to get away, but rather hit him or her with a series of quick blows to the shins, knees, groin, solar plexus, and chin.

Keep your opponent confused and wear him or her down by varying the speed and direction of your attacks. Circle the opponent and attack from an angle. Only charge directly forward when there is a clear opening to exploit. Try to use a decisive technique that will force an opponent to give up.

An opponent may try to confuse you by pretending to slow down his or her attack and lure you in for a set of surprise blows. To test an opponent's reaction, attack from an angle and retreat. If the opponent is tired or hurt, he or she will not be able to respond with long-range blows. Tire out an adversary by making him or her move, and work around behind him or her so that you can attack the sensitive areas. You may be able to execute a blow or perform a takedown that will end the fight.

### Taller and Weaker Attacker

A taller but weaker opponent will still have the advantage of longer limbs to hit with from a distance, so whenever possible, stay out of reach of his or her blows.

When you are stronger than a taller opponent, attack him or her along the centerline with direct straight-line attacks. Once you have slipped in close to your adversary, get your arms inside his or her arms. Keeping your head tucked in and your elbows close to your body, punch the opponent using the motion of your hips to increase the force. A smaller opponent can defeat an adversary by slipping in under his or her defenses and delivering a series of hard and concentrated blows to sensitive areas. If there is not a clear

shot at the opponent's front centerline, move in at an angle or circle to the rear to attack.

If your opponent is careful to avoid leaving openings, draw him or her out by pretending to move in, only to step aside and attack with a combination of close blows. Some taller opponents keep their guard up as they pick off an opponent with long-range attacks. Try to lower a taller opponent's guard by executing left hooks to the body from close range. When the opponent's guard is lowered, immediately throw high punches. If a taller person tries to clinch you to catch a breath, use the opportunity to get at him or her with punches to the centerline.

If you are sure of your grappling abilities, try to get in close for a takedown to end the fight. When in close, hit the opponent hard with a series of blows, then move to perform a takedown or apply a hold. If your opponent is successful in getting away from your grip, then move out and circle. At close range your opponent's reach advantage is neutralized and he or she will have a difficult time evading your moves. Try to back the opponent into a corner where he or she cannot avoid your repeated blows to sensitive areas and/or your takedown maneuver.

## More Powerful Attacker of the Same Height

When fighting a person who is the same height as you but more powerful, never let him or her know that you think you may be weaker. Instead, show your confidence and your ability to react quickly by throwing lead blows, such as a left jab, backfist, or front kick, to keep the opponent at a distance. If you are sure an opponent is truly stronger, then you do not want to be at a range where you run the risk of being punched or grabbed. Never slug it out with someone who is more powerful. Unless an opponent's centerline is clearly open, attack at an angle or after you have circled to the rear, so that you are in a fairly safe place when executing your blows. Be careful not to allow an opponent to back you into a corner where he or she can get in close to rain blows on you or wrestle you to the ground.

If an opponent charges, step off to the side to throw him or her off balance, and follow through with a combination of blows. If this does not end the fight, keep your opponent at bay with well-timed jabs, forcing him or her to keep weight on the rear leg in a defensive position. From this position, the opponent may not be able to easily use his or her weight to throw powerful punches.

If the opponent tries to clinch you, hit hard with a series of uppercuts, hook punches, knee attacks, elbow strikes, or short kicks to sensitive areas. Do not let an opponent draw you in close so that he or she can grab you. End a fight with a stronger opponent by throwing a series of blows from an area that you believe is safe, or by executing a quick hold, lock, or throw after the opponent is obviously weakened and off balance.

## Shorter and More Powerful Attacker

Take advantage of your longer reach when dealing with a shorter, more powerful adversary. This type of opponent may depend heavily on powerful hook punches. You cannot evade these blows by simply moving backward because the hook may hit you before you can move back out of the way. Instead, avoid the blow by moving around so that each time the opponent throws a hook punch, he or she is off balance. Never try to match similar blows with a more powerful person who throws hook punches. Throw straight punches that will allow your blow to get to the target faster than the hooks.

Watch an opponent's balance carefully. If a wild swinging punch misses, deflect it and grab the arm that was used to attack, using the opponent's momentum to direct him or her further off balance. From a position at the opponent's side, use your grip and his or her lack of balance to start an attack by hitting the opponent with a quick series of blows and then moving out of attacking range. Do not let the opponent get in close to your body where his or her superior power in punching or grappling will be an advantage.

If a shorter but stronger adversary gets close enough to grab you, force him or her back with a strong series of uppercuts, elbow strikes, knee attacks, or kicks to the shins. If you are put in a clinch, grab the opponent by the shoulders, and, keeping your arms inside the opponent's, bring your hands down onto his or her biceps. Attempt a tripping action or pull away quickly and hit with a long-range blow if the opponent is off balance. The clinch must be broken quickly in order to get distance between you and the opponent so that he or she cannot resume close-range fighting.

In a prolonged fight, be extremely mobile and wear your opponent down with a strong set of straight blows from a distance. To keep the opponent at bay, put a lead punch or kick between you. Do not throw a kick higher than stomach level or you may be off balance and vulnerable to a takedown. Surprise the opponent by following up a lead with a hook punch. Try to execute a decisive technique.

Use your longer reach to keep an adversary at bay while you execute blows to take the aggression out of him or her. If the opponent charges, side step and counterattack. Mix your attacks, and approach directly and from an angle. At times, move forward at an angle as though you were going to pass your opponent and punch. Hit your opponent as he or she changes body position or moves to cross ranges.

## Attacker of Same Height and Power

When confronting an attacker equal to you in height and power, seize the psychological edge by assuming the attitude that you are the stronger and more skilled. Keep moving to avoid being a stationary target.

Take advantage immediately of any openings by moving in with an attack. If you do not see any openings, fake a jab to test your opponent's reaction. Once you figure out the aggressor's weakness, try to use a decisive technique against it. Perform a mix of front, side, and charging attacks. Vary your combinations to keep that person confused as to what you are going to do next.

Some opponents of the same size may assume a strong defensive stance and rely on blocks and counterattacks. This type of adversary will often try to hit you after you execute your first technique and before you can throw a second. Make the defensive adversary move by attacking from odd angles that force him or her to change body position. Use fakes to throw off the opponent's timing, making him or her commit to a movement that will create an opening you can use to attack.

Until you are ready to move into close range, keep an aggressive opponent away with lead techniques. Fake low and then strike to close distance with your opponent. Once you sense that the aggressor is tired or is slowing down, increase the pressure with a series of fast attacks. To neutralize a potential blow and put a tired aggressor off balance, push hard against his or her shoulder as he or she is about to throw a punch. Use blocks that turn the opponent away and remove the attacking limb from between you. Once the attacking limb is temporarily neu-

tralized, you may move to apply a hold.

Force an opponent of similar size and power to fight in the style in which he or she is weakest. For example, if he or she wants to box, then you should wrestle. If an opponent is confused and forced to fight in an uncomfortable way, he or she may become discouraged enough to want to end the confrontation.

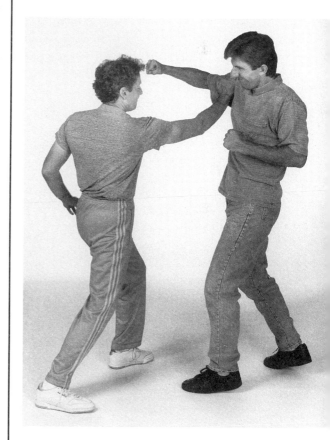

## Shorter and Weaker Attacker

Never allow an opponent's smaller size or lack of strength to lull you into a false sense of security. Such an adversary may be skilled enough to defeat you. Initially keep this type of opponent at a long distance. Stand tall to get the greatest psychological edge out of your height and make it difficult for your smaller opponent to reach your head. Throw kicks that will use up the aggressor's energy when blocked.

A smaller attacker will try to wear you out with hard blows from close range. Show confidence and keep a lead technique between the two of you. Force your opponent into a corner, and slowly cut off the area in which he or she can move. Then make contact with long-range punches and kicks—keeping the opponent on the defensive by varying the

rhythm, tempo, and pattern of your blows. Throw a hook from outside the opponent's line of vision by leading with a jab and then throwing a hook directly afterward with the same arm. Combine steady forward pressure with occasional quick charging moves.

If you sense that an opponent is weakening, decide whether you want to wrestle or to continue wearing the opponent down with blows or use a decisive technique. Do not allow the opponent to circle you, but use lateral movements to try to limit the space in which he or she can move. When your opponent tries to side step, hit hard with straight-line punches. If your opponent seems to move backward to avoid your blows, confuse him or her by suddenly changing the range of attack. For example, if your opponent expects attacks from close range, catch him or her off guard with a long-range attack. When an adversary is skilled at evading your attacks, use confusing types of movement to position yourself behind him or her. Then catch the adversary off guard with a swift combination of techniques, perhaps including a takedown.

A smaller aggressor may attempt to move into close range and penetrate your defenses with a series of strong blows. When you see him or her closing distance, quickly force him or her back with a series of blows. If the opponent holds back by staying in long range, draw him or her out by moving forward and then back. Then, as the opponent begins to move forward, quickly perform a surprise forward attack. If the opponent manages to get close and you do not want to grapple, push him or her away, or use knee attacks, kicks, elbow strikes, uppercut punches, or short vertical punches to drive the opponent back. When a smaller aggressor charges, you may side step the attack and hit him or her with a short punch to the side of the body.

If you do want to grapple, perform a takedown when your opponent has been weakened and is off balance. You can also perform a takedown from a clinch. Do not try to rest in a clinch when the aggressor can use his or her shorter arms to deliver powerful blows against you. Use the clinch only to wrestle your opponent into submission or to catch him or her off guard with a knee attack or a similar type of technique.

## HANDLING DIFFERENT PERSONALITY TYPES

An aggressor may not always fight as you might expect someone with his or her general physical characteristics to fight, so you must also consider other factors when determining your strategy. For example, even though an opponent may be taller and weaker, he or she may be foolish enough to move into close range in an attempt to intimidate you. That person would then be operating in a range in which he or she is especially weak. A skilled fighter who is taller and weaker would stay at a distance.

Your opponent's personality will influence his or her fighting style. In this section, we will look at several personality types common among fighters and suggest some ways of dealing with them. Most real-life opponents will show a mixture of these personality traits, so you have to judge each opponent individually. Use your own judgment in determining which characteristics match your opponent's.

### The Annoyer

The annoyer is not necessarily interested in a prolonged physical confrontation, but simply enjoys making you feel uncomfortable. This type of opponent may get discouraged if you do not seem to be bothered by his or her behavior. When the annoyer teases or taunts you, ignore him or her and move away, but do not turn your back—just in case he or she is tempted to attack you by surprise.

If the annoyer moves toward you, use simple self-defense maneuvers. Do not allow your temper to rule you. Use force only if the annoyer starts a physical confrontation. If at all possible, stay away from the annoying person.

## The Bully

A bully enjoys pushing weaker people around but really has very little confidence. Make sure you do not allow him or her to sense weakness in you. Show strong and confident determination without being overly defiant, but do not try to impress a bully by bragging.

If you do not sense potential aggression from a bully, laugh it off and walk away. If you sense, however, that the bully's unfriendly shove may lead to something more serious, watch for an opportunity to attack: a break in the bully's balance, any openings for attack at sensitive areas, or a chance to apply a lock. If the bully pushes you, pull him or her forward and follow through with a throw. If the aggressor pulls, push him or her into a vulnerable position. Using an attacker's energy against him or her will often bring an end to the bullying.

## The Wrestler

A wrestler often takes pride in his or her physique and ability to intimidate and control other people. The wrestler needs to be able to grab you and direct a fight, so movement and evasion on your part may make him or her extremely uncomfortable. If a confrontation begins, evade an initial attack and follow through with a counterattack. Move around and try to stay at long range so that you can hit the wrestler without being grabbed by him or her. A wrestler will often keep his or her hands high enough to grab you, leaving his or her lower body open. Take the fight out of the opponent with hard low kicks at knee level or lower.

Be ready to side step if the wrestler lunges at you. Do not depend on one punch to end the fight because a determined grappler is willing to take a powerful punch in order to get close to you. Exploit any clear opportunity to hit sensitive areas along the centerline with a series of combinations. Once you find a weak spot, keep hitting at that spot until the opponent's determination weakens. Direct most of your blows to the side or rear of the wrestler's body so that you do not put yourself within reach. If the opponent does close in, use elbows, uppercuts, or kicks to the shin to defend, but never throw high kicks that will leave you off balance—especially when dealing with a grappler.

Once a wrestler has you in a hold, you must move quickly to get a grip on that person's thumb or another finger to bend it back for a release. Watch the wrestler's hand position carefully, and exploit any weakness by applying a wristlock. You may also strike at or pinch sensitive areas on the body. A pinch

side and hitting the aggressor with strong counterpunches, and then withdrawing. Do not stand directly in front of the whirlwind puncher and attempt to exchange punches, hoping one of yours will hit that person's vulnerable centerline.

If you are confident in your grappling abilities, you may choose to move behind the whirlwind puncher and execute a takedown. From a rear position you will be difficult to hit, and an aggressive puncher will be very vulnerable. When you are caught in a clinch with the whirlwind puncher, hit him or her hard with a series of short blows and then withdraw. You may also use a clinch as an opportunity to perform a takedown or apply a hold or lock. Wild punchers have a tendency to wear out quickly because they are unprepared for prolonged combat, so if you are able to get beyond the initial attack, you will have a good chance for success.

in a tender area can force even a confident grappler to release a hold. If you are grabbed, keep moving, do not get discouraged, and work out a strategy that will allow you to move away.

### The Whirlwind Puncher

Some aggressors, especially bullies who are angry or upset, take out frustration by attacking people with a series of whirlwind punches. If you are dealing with a whirlwind puncher, stay in an area that has plenty of room for you to move. Do not attempt to get up close to talk. This kind of adversary is often unreasonable and unwilling to compromise, so avoiding him or her is best.

If it is not possible to avoid attack, take defensive action. Shoot a hard low kick at the aggressor's groin or kneecap to stop an advance, or evade a punch by moving to the

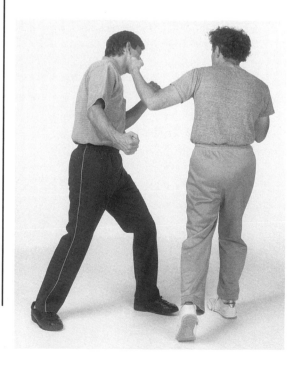

### The Powerhouse Knockout King

The powerhouse knockout king is the type of person who takes great pride in having an impressive body. At the beginning of a confrontation, he or she will often pose while telling you how easy it would be to pound you into the ground. Never let loose talk or big muscles intimidate you, because big muscles do not necessarily deliver powerful punches. Besides, even a powerful punch is harmless if it does not make contact.

Stay out of range of the powerhouse aggressor as an initial defense. Evade any blow, move around, and try to keep a lead technique between you and the opponent. When the powerhouse knockout king prepares to launch a punch, hit him or her first with a straight punch or kick. If that person completes a blow that misses you, follow through with a series of combinations. Catch the opponent by surprise, and execute blows to the side or rear of the opponent. When the knockout king charges with a punch, side step the attack and kick him or her from the side at an angle. Avoid using blocks (which absorb energy), and evade or parry blows whenever possible. Above all, do not stand in a direct line with the powerhouse knockout king and try to slug it out or grapple.

In any prolonged confrontation, get the psychological and physical edge by wearing the powerhouse knockout king down. Stay at a safe distance and evade attacking blows while taking advantage of angle attacks to weak spots on the opponent's body. If the opponent charges, move aside and counterattack. You may also use the opponent's momentum against him or her for a takedown, if you are confident of your grappling skills. You may defeat the powerhouse knockout king with a decisive technique or persistence.

## The Fancy-Footwork Ace

Influenced by martial-arts movies, a group of show-offs have emerged who can be characterized as fancy-footwork aces. These people have little or no training in martial arts, but they take great pride in being able to imitate the fancy kicks shown in the movies. If you show little interest in the opponent's display, he or she may go bother someone else.

If you are forced into a confrontation with a fancy-footwork ace, remember that kicks can only do harm by actually making contact with your body. Minimize the opportunity for such leg maneuvers to hit you by staying at close range where foot techniques cannot build power. The fancy-footwork ace often dreads close-range fighting, so force him or her into close range, where you can attack the centerline of the body. If the opponent manages to move off to the side, work your way around until you can move in close. Keep your hands high to protect your head while in close range, and stay at angles where you cannot easily be kicked. If the opponent turns his or her back on you while attempting a kick, close in quickly and perform a takedown.

When the fancy-footwork ace begins to throw high kicks, throw him or her off balance by moving to the side and then rushing in with a series of strong blows. Attack the opponent before or after he or she throws a kick, and remember that the fancy kicker is especially vulnerable right after a kick has missed. Discourage further kicks by following through (after dodging) with your own kick to the aggressor's supporting leg. A kicking ace often enjoys throwing kicks but is not good at defending against them.

## The Well-Balanced Fighter

Most of the aggressors you run into will have a limited range of abilities, because skilled fighters usually gravitate toward organized sports or martial arts, where they can take advantage of their skills. They find little need to prove themselves in street fighting. But it is possible that you will find yourself challenged by someone who actually has some fighting skill. Do not allow yourself to be intimidated.

First of all, refuse to be suckered into making the first move. The well-balanced fighter may want you to make a mistake so that he or she can make you look foolish by putting you away with a simple maneuver. If you remain calm and force him or her into making the first move, he or she may just give up.

However, if a fight starts, defend yourself. Gauge the opponent's strengths and weaknesses. If your adversary's weaknesses are not obvious, try to confuse him or her with fakes and combinations until you can spot a weakness to exploit. Some polished fighters may begin the fight by suddenly charging forward with an explosive attack that gives them a psychological advantage and puts body weight and momentum on their side. Defend either by evading the attack at an angle or by exploding forward with your own techniques. Timing is very important in a counterattack, so if you do not feel quick enough to catch a charging aggressor off guard, take a half step to the rear and then push forward to attack his or her exposed areas.

Be careful if your adversary assumes an opposite stance—one in which, contrary to most stances, the right side of his or her body is forward. (Such a position might be maintained throughout the confrontation, or your opponent might alternate forward sides to throw your strategy off by forcing you to face first one side and then the other.) Some opponents will do this to confuse you. Others prefer a right-forward stance because they are left-handed. In either case, if your left side and your opponent's right side are forward, circle away from that person's left (rear) hand while keeping your guard up against his or her right hooks.

If your opponent leads with a right jab off the forward arm, you can best evade it by moving to your left. This will put you outside the attacker's guard, where he or she cannot easily hit you with another blow—especially not with a powerful left-hand blow. (This blow will be especially powerful if your opponent is left-handed.) Then counterattack. If you evade to your right—to the inside of the opponent's guard—be ready with your right arm to block a powerful blow from your opponent's left hand. You may also parry the opponent's right jabs with your left hand and counterattack with your own right straight punch to the head. Watch out for circular

attacks off your opponent's rear side. Some opponents will assume an opposite stance in order to launch a powerful roundhouse kick off the rear leg to hit you at the vulnerable centerline. If an opponent seems slightly uncomfortable in a right-forward position, try to get him or her to lead. If your opponent leads with a right jab, evade it and catch him or her by surprise with a left hook thrown over the right lead blow. Again, keep your right arm ready to block a left punch.

If your opponent is proud of being able to block and counter your techniques, make him or her uncomfortable by attacking from unexpected angles, especially from positions where he or she cannot hit you with blows off the rear side. If your opponent relies on evasive movements to avoid your blows, vary the type and tempo of the movements you use to bring yourself in range to hit him or her. Use fakes, try to work your way around behind your opponent, and try other ways of catching him or her off guard.

Do not get locked into a pattern of fighting that will reveal your strengths and weaknesses. Also, emphasize a fighting style with which your opponent is uncomfortable. If he or she likes boxing, for example, emphasize grappling.

Do not try to match a polished fighter's speed. Instead, circle the opponent to neutralize his or her advantage. Move to the side and hit from long range with lead techniques such as a left jab or front kick. Analyze all of the attacker's reactions and then follow through accordingly with appropriate blows. Like the ninja warriors, you will have to adapt to the situation by using all your natural advantages.

# 12

# SAFETY CONSIDERATIONS FOR PRACTICE

The techniques taught in this book will only be effective if you learn, understand, and practice them so that you can use them naturally and without hesitation in a real confrontation. Learn and practice commando techniques under the supervision of a qualified instructor. Do not simply sign up for the first class you find, but research and visit possible classes in commando training. Observe a training session and talk with people who are in the class to see how they like it. Once you have found a class that you feel is right for you, attend it regularly.

Do not practice fighting techniques on your family or friends. This can be very dangerous. Practice fighting techniques only under the supervision of your instructor. You may choose to use this book as a supplement for your training. In using it as a guidebook for practice, it is important to follow the suggestions listed below.

1. Do not start a class until you are examined by your doctor and have his or her approval. Get regular medical checkups to make sure that you can handle strenuous physical training.

2. Before executing any fighting techniques, make sure that your body is warmed

up. Start with a relaxing walk. Then begin a slow set of stretching exercises. Make sure all the major parts of your body are thoroughly stretched and warmed up.

3. When practicing, begin slowly and concentrate on form. Once you are sure that your form is adequate, you can slowly increase your speed.

4. Stay loose and limber while practicing martial-arts techniques. When you are tense, you slow down and tire out more quickly.

5. Practice combinations of techniques so that one technique flows into the next.

6. Try to practice fighting techniques in front of a mirror to get an idea of what they look like. This will help improve your form.

7. While practicing, always wear safety equipment such as a headguard, mouthpiece, groin-cup, knee guards, and any other protective gear needed. When working on punches and kicks with a partner, you should wear, in addition to all of this safety equipment, padded gloves, shinguards, and protective coverings for your feet. Any grappling should be practiced on a thick mat designed for wrestling.

8. When practicing with a partner, do not put all of your force into a punch. Stop your blows at least one inch from your partner. Only very advanced practitioners with approval from their instructors are allowed to make any contact. The instructor should be present to supervise the practice session. *Practice full-power techniques only on a punching bag—not on a human being.*

9. Do not make contact with your training partner unless he or she agrees to it, you are both wearing FULL safety equipment, and you are supervised by your instructor. During practice, never hit sensitive areas on your partner, such as the eyes, nose, throat, neck, ribs, groin, knees, or any area along the centerline on the rear of the body. Do not even pretend to throw blows to such sensitive areas on a practice partner.

10. Do not try to imitate the training methods of advanced martial artists. They are conditioned and trained to deal with situations that you are not ready to handle. Avoid doing anything other than what you have been specifically taught to do. Practice under supervision and with proper safety precautions.

11. Concentrate on developing a strong foundation in basic self-defense techniques. Avoid flashy techniques, such as high kicks, that leave you off balance.

12. Remember to squeeze your fist together tightly just before hitting something. This will help protect your hand and wrist.

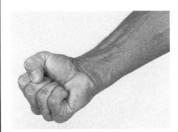

13. Never surprise your training partner with a throw, sweep, lock, or hold, and be sure that your partner is ready to start before executing these techniques. Do not practice any technique with someone who does not understand what is required for self-protection. Make sure a qualified instructor explains and demonstrates any new techniques to you and your partner. Treat all training partners with respect and consideration for their safety.

14. Practice falling techniques under the guidance of a qualified instructor. Make sure you can successfully perform all falls before you allow anyone to throw you. Likewise, do not throw a practice partner unless he or she has excellent falling skills. All falling during throwing practice should be done on a safety mat. Do not throw a practice partner or let yourself be thrown unless you are under an instructor's supervision.

15. Make sure that you and your partner are thoroughly warmed up, well stretched, and loose before applying any locking techniques or holds. Work out a warning system with your partner to signal when to release a hold or lock that becomes painful. Never practice any locks on a part of the body that is sore, weak, or has a history of serious injury.

16. Practice falling, holds, locks, grappling, or throws only under the supervision of a qualified martial-arts instructor.

# Index

## About the Author

Fred Neff started his training in the Asian fighting arts at the age of eight. In 1974, Mr. Neff received a rank of fifth degree black belt in karate. The same year he was made a master of the art of kempo at a formal ceremony. He is also proficient in judo, jujutsu, and more than one style of chuan-fa. Mr. Neff's study of East Asian culture has taken him to Hong Kong, Japan, the People's Republic of China, and Singapore.

For many years, Mr. Neff has used his knowledge to educate others. He has taught karate at the University of Minnesota, the University of Wisconsin, Hamline University, and Inver Hills Community College in St. Paul, Minnesota. He has also organized and supervised self-defense classes for special education programs, public schools, private institutions, and city recreation departments. Included in his teaching program have been classes for law enforcement officers.

He has received many awards for his accomplishments and active community involvement, including the City of St. Paul Citizen of the Month Award in 1975, a Commendation for Distinguished Service from the Sibley County Attorney's Office in 1980, the WCCO Radio Good Neighbor Award in 1985, the Lamp of Knowledge Award from the Twin Cities Lawyers Guild in 1986, and the Presidential Medal of Merit in 1990.

Fred Neff graduated with high distinction from the University of Minnesota College of Education in 1970. In 1976, he received his J.D. degree from William Mitchell College of

Law in St. Paul, Minnesota. Mr. Neff is a practicing attorney in Minneapolis, Minnesota.

He is the author of 19 books, including *Everybody's Book of Self-Defense, Lessons from the Western Warriors, Lessons from the Eastern Warriors, Lessons from the Japanese Masters,* and the eight books that make up Fred Neff's Self-Defense Library.